Bible Study for Pagans

Fred Nichols

Copyright © 2013 Fred Nichols

All rights reserved

Table of Contents

Bible Study for Pagans

Preface

The Old Testament

Introduction

Genesis

The Book of Exodus

The Book of Leviticus

The Book of Numbers

The Book of Deuteronomy

The Book of Joshua

The Book of Judges

The Book of Ruth

The First & Second Books of Samuel

The First & Second Books of the Kings

The First and Second Books of the Chronicles

The Book of Ezra and Nehemiah

Esther

The Book of Job

The Psalms

The Book of Proverbs

Ecclesiastes

The Song of Songs

The Book of Isaiah

Jeremiah

Lamentations

Ezekiel

Daniel

The Minor Prophets

The New Testament

Introduction

The Gospel According to Saint Mark

The Gospel According to Saint Matthew

The Gospel According to Saint Luke

The Gospel According to Saint John

Acts of the Apostles

The Letters of Saint Paul

The Letter of James

1 Peter

1, 2 & 3 John

The Letter of Jude

The Book of Revelation

Preface

As a young man, I worked the nightshift at a postal processing center in Sacramento. There I ran into a subculture of fundamentalist Christians who brought their Bibles to work and never tired of trying to save the rest of us ignorant pagans during our lunch half-hour. They weren't aggressive or impolite about it, just letting the chance "Praise the Lord" and "Thank you, Jesus" slip into their conversation from time to time, always ready for someone to react or ask a question.

And it's hard *not* to ask a question when a man you've worked with side-by-side for years removes his steaming cheeseburger from the microwave and murmurs "Thank you, Jesus." If you then ask what Jesus could possibly have to do with it, you've opened—not Pandora's Box; that's a pagan expression—no, something far worse: you've opened the Bible.

I admit it: I asked for it. I asked the kind of skeptical questions a bored non-believer working the nightshift might be expected to ask. Naturally, I became an opportunity for salvation.

To defend myself, I began reading the Bible, which of course was exactly what my fundamentalist friends wanted me to do. But my reaction wasn't what they were hoping for. What I found in there wasn't *anything* like the hallelujah stuff they were preaching to me. From the outset, it seemed clear to me that the Bible was a Jewish family album, with the strange adventures of a rebellious Son tacked on at the end.

I determined to stick with it, to see if I couldn't complete the cover-to-cover journey, like an intrepid British adventurer walking the length of darkest Africa.

Much of what I found in there is, in its way, magnificent. The Old Testament—the struggle for survival of the Jews, with its honest admissions of their shortcomings, is a great epic story. But it's not a single, continuous narrative. It's more like a patchwork of stories and legends and lessons gathered over the course of centuries and skillfully sewn together—but with the seams showing nevertheless.

The comedy—and there's plenty of it—comes not so much from the material itself as from the effort to force it into the guise of a single inspired utterance from the Creator, every word of it golden. Generations of rabbi-editors worked at this task, and you can almost see them behind Yahweh's great booming pronouncements and exhortations—a hoard of little Ozs scuttling around in the background yanking on levers and adjusting pulleys.

Then there's the New Testament and Jesus—a complex, intimidating, sometimes sweet man. All we know of him is from the four snapshots known as the Gospels.

Finally, Paul, the inventor of Christianity. What an administrator he was! What a visionary! What a politician! Wait until you see.

Enjoy.

The Old Testament

Introduction

The quest for Jewish national and cultural identity began in about 1750 BCE with the migration of Abraham and his household from Mesopotamia to Canaan (roughly the area that we now call Palestine). About a thousand years later it looked like the great Jewish adventure was at an end. In 587 BCE the king of Babylon, Nebuchadnezzar II, demolished Jerusalem, conquered Judea, and sent most of the survivors to Babylon.

Once they were exiled to Babylon, the greatest dangers for the Jewish people were the pressures of assimilation that threatened to dilute and dissipate their cultural identity. To save this culture, to keep the people from straying away from their ethnic and religious roots, their priests set about to collect and write down their history and codify their religion. The product of this effort is the Old Testament. It is, in the main, the history of the Jews from about 1750 BCE to the last years of the Babylonian exile, around 530 BCE.

No one knows who the editor/authors of the Old Testament were, or over how long a period of time it took to assemble this great document. But clearly it was not done all at once. It seems to have passed through the hands of a number of priestly scholars, not all of whom were of the same persuasion as to exactly what it meant to be a Jew. Scholars have identified three separate traditions: J, E, and P. "J" is for the sections of the narrative that use the name Jehovah (or Yahweh) to refer to God, and "E" is for the sections that refer to God as Elohim. "P" is for the priestly writers who strained to pull all this material together into a more or less cohesive whole and point it in the direction of what they believed was correct doctrine. The narrative tributaries of the J and E editors/authors are older than that of the P, with E perhaps containing the most ancient material and also contributing by far the least content.

Though the superstructure of the Old Testament is the history of the Jews, it encompasses as well books of prophecy, poetry, and a handful of adventure stories that seem mainly intended to entertain.

By far the most important books of the Old Testament are the first five—*Genesis, Exodus, Leviticus, Numbers,* and *Deuteronomy.* Called by Christians the Pentateuch, to the Jews they are known as the Torah, the sacred heart of the Jewish faith. The core of Jewish history and all its laws are found here. Countless generations of Jewish scholars have spent their whole lives poring over the meaning of the Torah.

We begin with Creation.

Genesis

Genesis is a sacred stew. More than any other book in the Bible, it lumps into a single pot ancient myths, ancient history, and the more or less "modern" perspectives of the Old Testament's last compilers.

The stories of Creation, Adam and Eve, the Flood, and Abraham don't flow as a continuous narrative. They're glued-together fragments that bump the narrative down the road. It isn't until well into Abraham's biography that the writing settles down into a cohesive account of the history of the Hebrews.

Right off, the Bible starts with a stutter. Two creation accounts clumsily abut each other. Everyone's familiar with the start of the first one:

> *In the beginning God created the heavens and the earth.*
> *1:1*

This version of creation was probably written by the priests of the P or Priestly tradition, as they sought to put a beginning to the story that sets the tone of God's dignified and orderly management of the universe. That first verse puts into motion the Seven Day Project of Creation, including light, firmament (a kind of bowl over the earth that keeps the sky from falling down), oceans and land, vegetation, the stars, fish and birds, land creatures, and finally one man and one woman. That takes six days, plus one to rest. With that, God checks Creation off the To Do list.

But then we encounter a second version of the creation story, starring Adam and Eve. It starts with bare land devoid of vegetation. God adds water, and suddenly life explodes all over the place. Next thing you know Adam and Eve are standing next to each other in the Garden of Eden. Oh boy, you know what's coming next.

Don't Do It!
Reading or, earlier in my life, hearing the story of Adam and Eve always made me feel a little sad and uncomfortable. Adam, mild, accommodating, not wishing to offend, comes off like a schmuck. Eve, resentful of her subordinate status (the only creature made from another creature and, moreover, appointed specifically to be a "helpmeet"), too readily seizes the first opportunity to gain a little leverage. You know how it goes: God lays down only one rule: "...of the tree of the knowledge of good and evil you are not to eat...." (2:17) As Adam and Eve wander around the Garden of Eden a serpent draws Eve's attention to the forbidden tree and its powers. She immediately sees what eating the fruit could mean. *We'll be gods!*

Out here in the audience I would squirm, wanting to call out "Wait! Think it over! Talk to God about it first!" But no, while Adam looks on, ox-like, knowing this is going to get them into big trouble, his tough wife takes the fateful bite. Then, still silent, wiping the juice from her lips, she offers the fruit to her husband. Mankind's miserable future is fixed.

But reading the story now I see it in a new light. This little tiff in the Garden is actually a great personal triumph for Yahweh. It proves that He's finally succeeded in inventing a creature who thinks for itself. At last! Here is a being that can *choose* not to obey Him, can choose not to worship Him. And if, after making this damnable mistake, this same being is willing to go through the struggle and suffering necessary to heal the breach, then God is getting the first outside affirmation that He really is as glorious and lovable as He'd always hoped He was.

No wonder Yahweh stays with these beings all through the Old Testament and beyond. Every time they defy Him, or blaspheme Him, or ignore Him, they're reaffirming their ability to act outside His will. They are his Chosen People because they alone have the ability to choose *Him*, and the drama is about whether or not they ultimately will. The suspense comes from the question of whether not Yahweh has the patience to wait until they make up their minds.

Cain and Abel

As everyone knows, after Adam and Eve are evicted from Eden, they have two sons, Cain and Abel, who go down different career paths: Abel "became a shepherd and kept flocks, while Cain tilled the soil." (4:2-3) When they make ritual offerings to Yahweh, the Deity prefers Abel's offering of the first-born of his flock to Cain's offering of produce. It's no surprise that Cain goes away feeling rejected and resentful.

So, why did Yahweh prefer the shepherd to the farmer? For one thing, a shepherd tending his flock is the presiding Biblical metaphor for God's relationship to man. But, more practically speaking, the Hebrews were a nomadic people. For centuries, dating back at least to the second millennium BCE, the peoples living on the fringes of established civilizations such as Egypt and Mesopotamia were lumped together under the generic term "'Apiru" or "Habiru," which easily morphs into "Hebrew."[1] They

---

[1] At this point they're Hebrews. Later they will be called Israelites, the

were nomads, tending flocks, interacting loosely with the civilizations they pitched their tents near. At this point in history the name Hebrew does not refer to an ethnically or religiously unified group. They were the gypsies of the Fertile Crescent.

The point is they wander for a living. If you add up all the generations listed in the genealogical section (Chapter 5), they're scheduled to be on the road for about eight thousand years. So agriculture was not a practical choice for them. Yet. Cain wasn't wrong, he was just ahead of his time. But he doesn't know that. Right now, he's just sulking. And the sulking festers. Before you know it, Cain has invented murder. Abel is dead, his blood crying out to Yahweh from the ground. When Yahweh pronounces His sentence—banishment—Cain cries out:

> *My punishment is greater than I can bear. See!*
> *Today you drive me from this ground. I must*
> *hide from you, and be a fugitive and a*
> *wanderer over the earth.*
> 4:13-14

There's some irony here—the would-be farmer is sentenced to lead the life of a nomad.

The Begats

The part of *Genesis* everybody dreads is the genealogy section, Chapter 5. More than one person has said to me, "I could never read the Old Testament—all that 'he *begat* him and he *begat* the other' stuff." Well, guess what? It's only one page! You can read

---

descendents of the patriarch Israel. Finally they are called Jews, which refers to Israelites living in Judah, the largest of the tribal areas in Canaan or the Promised Land. It can be confusing!

it in the time it takes to eat a donut.

The genealogies end with Noah, which will get us into the story of the Flood. But first, there is a curious and disturbing interlude titled "Sons of God and daughters of men."

The Nephilim
It's only one paragraph, and hardly anybody talks about it, but what it says is pretty hard to get around: *Yahweh allowed His angels to raid the earth for sex.* This occurred at about the same time that Yahweh was deciding to trash the whole mankind experiment anyway ("Yahweh regretted having made man on earth..." [6:6]), so maybe He didn't mind that all this disgusting stuff was going on. Here it is:

> *"...the sons of God, looking at the daughters of men, saw they were pleasing, so they married as many as they chose... the sons of God resorted to the daughters of man, and had children by them. These are the heroes of days gone by, the famous men.*
> 6:2-4

These unions resulted in a race of giants called Nephilim. We will run into them again in *Numbers*, when they frighten a scouting party of Hebrew warriors ("We felt like grasshoppers," they say). It's fun to speculate that if giants like these had really existed, other cultures might have given them names like Hercules and Perseus.

Noah and the Flood
Now, just as Yahweh is on the point consigning this whole messy Creation to oblivion, one man—Noah—stands between Him and

the annihilation of humanity. Because the story of Noah and the Flood is a fable, there's no use subjecting it to a lot scrutiny and interpretation. You may want to ask questions like "Why, when Yahweh decided that the sight of mankind disgusted Him, was it necessary to destroy nearly every living thing on the earth? I mean, what was the tufted titmouse doing that was so terrible?"—but it would be inappropriate. A grand gesture of near-total destruction was required, and that's all the explanation we need.

Yahweh made a covenant with Noah—the First Covenant—that He would never flood the earth again.

Anyway, the story of Noah and the Flood, and the little anecdote that follows of the Tower of Babel, are just warm-up acts for the saga of Abraham and the subsequent singling out of his descendents as the Chosen People. Here the glow of fable recedes and the graininess of sacred history begins to push forward.

Patriarch of the Israelites
When Yahweh first spoke to him in about 1750 BCE, Abraham, a descendent of Noah, was living in Ur (Lower Mesopotamia) as the head of a Hebrew family. Yahweh's first words to him are these: "Leave your country, your family and your father's house, for the land I will show you." (12:1) The land Yahweh was referring to, of course, was Canaan (Palestine), where Abraham managed to establish a Hebrew outpost in the southern desert. He was successful enough there, but he hardly took the place over. The Canaanites tolerated him and did business with him and allowed him to become wealthy. When he was very old and his son Isaac was ready to marry, Abraham sent a servant back to Mesopotamia to find his son a bride. The success of this mission triggered another wave of Hebrew migration across the Fertile Crescent...and so on.

That is the essence of Abraham's story. But the drama is in how Yahweh made himself known to these people, now that He had decided to insert Himself in their history. This the editors give to us in a series of loosely-linked anecdotes, some of which are meant to instruct, others to give the reader a sense of historical linkage with ancient events, and others merely to inspire awe.

Take Her, She's my Sister

This is definitely meant to be an instructive story. Sometime after Abraham arrived in Canaan, a famine beset the land (12:10) and he is forced to take his household to Egypt in search of food. As Abraham's caravan approaches the border, he becomes anxious about his wife Sarah—not for her safety, but for his own.

> *"Listen!* [he says to Sarah] *I know you are a beautiful woman. When the Egyptians see you they will say, 'That is his wife,' and they will kill me but spare you. Tell them you are my sister, so that they may treat me well because of you..."*

12:11-12

Obviously, chivalry hasn't been invented yet. Pharaoh reacts as Abraham predicted. To his credit, he is good-hearted enough to make Abraham a rich man in return for the use of his "sister." But no one had asked Yahweh about this arrangement, and He didn't like it. Suddenly Pharaoh discovers he has a plague problem (12:17), and quickly figures out what the cause is. He returns Sarah to Abraham, and though he complains bitterly about the ruse and expels them from the land, he is still intimidated enough to let Abraham keep all of his goods. Later Abraham will pull the same stunt with Abimelech, a Philistine king, with similar success.

The lesson? *Swallow your pride, do what you have to do to survive, and God will take care of the rest.*

The Second Covenant
This story falls into the historical linkage category, I suppose, giving some sacred resonance to the practice of circumcision, which in my opinion needs a *lot* of explaining.

Abraham's special gift was to know exactly whose voice he was hearing in his head. In those days there were gods all over the place, and even in Abraham's family it wasn't unusual to keep an idol in the household as a sort of good luck charm. But when God approaches Abraham for the first time, Abraham immediately knows who is tapping him on the shoulder: This isn't just some fertility or weather god, this is the Big Guy, the Creator, Yahweh. And when Yahweh says "All your males must be circumcised," (17:11) Abraham's only thought was to get out his knife.

Practically speaking, there was probably some principle of desert hygiene behind it all, though Abraham's lack of interest in explanations is exactly the quality that endears him to Yahweh. After first circumcising himself (ouch!) Abraham presumably begins calling men to his tent and cutting their penises too.

Not until Yahweh sends His own Son down to intercede for mankind will He again deal with a human being so satisfyingly obedient as Abraham (and even Jesus protests a couple of times).

Guess Who's Coming to Dinner?
Abraham had fulfilled his part of the covenant. Yahweh's end of the deal was to give Abraham a son. "I will bless [Sarah] and nations shall come out of her; kings of peoples shall descend from her." (17:16)

This proclamation could have been like a thundering, earth-shaking Ten Commandments moment, but here the editors decided to soften and humanize it: "Abraham bowed to the ground, and he laughed, thinking to himself, 'Is a child to be born to a man one hundred years old, and will Sarah have a child at the age of ninety?'" (17:17-18)

Later, Sarah gets her chance to react to the news in what is the most charming domestic scene in all of the Bible. Abraham has set up camp at a place called the Oak of Mamre. Sitting by the entrance of his tent in the heat of the day, he must have dozed off, because suddenly Yahweh is standing in front of him, accompanied by two angels. Abraham comically scrambles to play the perfect host. He seats his divine visitors under the oak tree and promises them refreshments in short order. Then he rushes back to the camp, where they are obviously unprepared for even the most casual of human visitors, and orders Sarah to "knead three bushels of flour and make loaves." He also selects a calf from his herd and gives orders for it to be slaughtered and prepared. Can you imagine how long this all must have taken? There is no hint that there was any divine assistance from Yahweh or the angels, only that presently Abraham was serving them veal, with milk and cream, and presumably bread too. Then they begin to discuss their business. Yahweh tells Abraham He's prepared to make good on His promise of Sarah bearing a child.

Sarah, hidden behind the entrance to the tent, is listening to all this. When she hears Yahweh promise to visit them again next year, to see Abraham's son, she laughs to herself: "Now that I am past the age of childbearing, and my husband is an old man, is pleasure to come my way again?" (18:13)

This, ladies and gentlemen, is the only reference to sexual pleasure in nearly 1700 pages of holy scripture. Yahweh overhears Sarah's giggles, and asks why she is laughing. "Is anything too wonderful for Yahweh?" growls the Deity, feigning displeasure and I'm sure scaring the shit out of everyone within earshot. "I did not laugh," says Sarah, frightened. "Oh yes, you did laugh," says Yahweh, ribbing her, letting His affection show.

Still smiling and shaking His head, Yahweh, Abraham, and the two angels walk to a hill overlooking Sodom, a place where they practice, er…*sodomy*. Guess what happens next.

Sodom and Gomorrah
This story would fall into the awe-inspiring category, I would think. It's a very satisfying vengeance story. After dinner with Abraham, the two angels stroll into Sodom in the evening, to investigate how bad things there have really gotten. Their cover story is that they've just come to spend the night and go on their way in the morning. Lot, Abraham's brother, spots them and knows them for what they are. He hastens to get them off the street and into his house, before the lewd and perverse townfolk get at them. But the word gets out, and soon Lot's house is surrounded by "the men of Sodom both young and old," who call out to Lot to send the strangers out so "that we may abuse them." (19:5)

You just know this is about to get good.

Lot heightens our anticipation by jumping up to play the ineffectual peacemaker. He offers the mob his two virgin daughters if they will only leave the strangers alone. 'No deal,' they say. 'We want the two lads,' and they push Lot aside and reach for the angels.

There's probably a place in Hell where they're still reaching. Everyone clamoring in Lot's doorway is struck blind. In the confusion that follows the angels turn to Lot and tell him to take his family and get out of town, right now, *this second.* When he hesitates, frightened and disoriented, they gently take him by the hand and lead him away. It's a nice touch, a little compassion, a little calm before the storm. The only sour note is what happens to Lot's wife who, contrary to instructions, turns to look once last time at the city and for this transgression is turned into a pillar of kosher salt.

Then the angels give Yahweh the high sign and He lets loose with the heavy artillery, pouring down fire and brimstone like there's no tomorrow. The nearby village of Gomorrah also is wiped off the face of the earth, though its citizens were never actually accused of anything. Probably one of those 'if you didn't know, you should have known' kind of deals.

Abraham returns to the desert plains of southern Canaan where, after playing the sister trick with Sarah on the local king, Abimelech, he settles down to raise his family. As promised, ninety-something Sarah has a son, Isaac.

The Sacrifice of Isaac
This little drama is regarded by some as the central event in *Genesis*, a metaphysical rhyme in which a father sacrificing his only son in the Old Testament foreshadows a Father sacrificing His only Son in the New Testament. (Of course, Abraham already had a son, Ishmael, by the ungrateful slave girl Hagar, but as a bastard he didn't count.)

"It happened some time later that God put Abraham to the test." (22:1) Yahweh always expects a lot in the Old Testament (less in the New), and His people are always coming up short, but this notion of a *test*—I believe Abraham is the only one so honored, unless you count Adam and Eve. As you'll recall, Yahweh learned from the Garden of Eden test that He had finally managed to create something with its own pushy will. Now apparently He wanted to learn if, among those creatures, there was one who would freely subdue his human wishes in favor of his Creator's.

The perfect test for this is to ask the subject to sacrifice—for no reason—something dear to the subject's heart.

Here's how it unfolds:

> *"Abraham, Abraham," He called.*
> *"Here I am," he replied.*
>
> *"Take your son," God said, "your only child Isaac, whom you love, and go to the land of Moriah. There you shall offer him as a burnt offering, on a mountain I will point out to you."*
> 22:2

Now a making a burnt offering doesn't just mean you build a big fire, throw something on it and walk away. According to the first chapter of *Leviticus* you must do the following: first you slit the victim's throat and pour out his blood on the altar; then you quarter his body, arranging the quarters, "as well as the head and the fat," on the wood pile; then you wash the legs and entrails in water, and place them on the pile; finally you light the fire, "and the fragrance of it will appease Yahweh." (*Leviticus* 1:13)

All of this Abraham agrees to do without hesitating in the slightest. He chops the wood, loads up a donkey, gets his knife and his little portable stove with a live coal inside, and tells Isaac to come with him.

Now it would be nice to think that, rather than dumb obedience, what Abraham was drawing upon here was a subtle well of knowledge about his God and techniques for appeasing Him. There are a couple of clues that this might be so. At the final campsite, as Abraham and Isaac are making ready to go up the hill to perform the ritual, Abraham turns to his servants and says "Stay here with the donkey. The boy and I will go over there; we will worship and come back to you." (22:5) Note that "we will come back." Does Abraham already know what's going to happen?

As they walk up the hill with Isaac, whom everybody imagines is about twelve, carrying the wood (omigod, almost like Jesus carrying his own cross!) father and son engage in what may be the most heart-rending dialogue in the whole Bible. Isaac speaks first:

> *"Father," he said.*
>
> *"Yes, my son," he replied.*
>
> *"Look," he said, "here are the fire and the wood, but where is the lamb for the burnt offering?"*
>
> *Abraham answered, "My son, God himself will provide the lamb for the burnt offering."*
> 22:7-8

"God himself will provide the lamb." That's clue number two that Abraham understood the game Yahweh is playing.

As Abraham raises the knife above his son Yahweh calls out to still his hand, wholly appeased. Abraham looks up to see a ram caught in the bushes nearby. As Abraham hoped, Yahweh has sent a new candidate for the sacrifice and the danger is past.

Maybe Abraham wasn't this clever. The straightforward reading of this story is that God was looking for an exceptionally obedient man upon whom to build Hebrew history, and that, having found one, He put him to a harsh test to make sure. But the people whose existence was ordained by Abraham's behavior are more notable for their cleverness and independence of thought than for their obedience to arbitrary rulers. Appeasement, yes—pander your wife to the Pharaoh, if that gets you through a season or two—but blind obedience? I don't think so.

In any case the test is administered and Abraham passes it and goes on to become a rich old man. When the time comes to find a wife for Isaac, Abraham is adamant about sending back to Mesopotamia for a nice Hebrew girl. The servant charged with this mission settles on a beauty named Rebekah, Abraham's great-niece from the family of his brother Nahor.

Here the narrative briefly passes on to Isaac, who is not a towering figure in Hebrew history. But Isaac does his job, which is to pass his genes on to Jacob, who *is* a towering figure.

Jacob the Trickster
If there is any question of whether or not (intentionally or not) Yahweh was selecting for cleverness when He settled on Abraham to be the Chosen People's patriarch, Jacob answers it. He is a trickster.

Remember that the essential function of the narrative at this point is to dramatize the migration of the Hebrew people from Lower Mesopotamia to Canaan under the prodding of a strange new God who was telling them they were His Chosen People.

There are some real ethical paradoxes in Jacob's story. There is, for example, the narrative's obvious approval of how Jacob deals with his older brother Esau. Esau is a big, hirsute outdoors type, a hunter, while smooth-skinned Jacob prefers to stay at home among the women and elders. The editors are setting up a classic competition between a person who lives by physical strength versus one who lives by his wits. You get the feeling that Jacob is more *Jewish* than Esau: he's closer to his mother, he's more cerebral. Esau, on the other hand, seems indifferent to the nuances of his culture.

In any case, Jacob to conspires with his mother to strip Esau of his primogenitive rights. The elements of this crime—the conspiracy between Jacob and his mother to disenfranchise Esau; the bald deceit of Jacob's impersonation of Esau; the obvious disdain in which the nearly senile Isaac is held by his wife and younger son—seem so obviously wrong—immoral, unjust, *unkind*—it's amazing that the narrative takes so much delight in presenting it.

Picture it: enfeebled, blind, Isaac sits in his darkened tent waiting to die. He cares only for the little things that make his waning years comfortable. He asks Esau to prepare his favorite "savory," probably something made from meat and spices. Isaac promises to formally bless him when he returns with it. Esau goes off to kill some game with which make the dish. In the meantime, Rebekah, who has overheard, hustles to get Jacob into the tent before Esau returns. She prepares the savory herself, from two goat kids, and tells Jacob to hurry and present it to the old man. Jacob worries that blind Isaac will touch him and know from his smooth skin that he is not Esau. Rebekah fixes that by wrapping him in the skins of the kids and pushes him into the dark tent.

"Father," he says, "I am Esau your first-born; I have done as you have told me." (27:18) Isaac falls for the ruse, blesses Jacob, and thus passes to him the leadership of the next generation.

At least the narrative recognizes that Esau has a right to be angry. Jacob flees for his life back to the old country in Mesopotamia, hoping that over time his brother's wrath will cool. While he waits he learns a lesson: he's not the only trickster in the tribe.

Laban the Deceitful
Jacob joins the household of his Uncle Laban, and goes to work tending Laban's herds. They negotiate a deal whereby Jacob will work for seven years in return for Laban's daughter Rachel. But when the time comes for Laban to give Rachel over, he sneaks his older and less appealing daughter Leah into Jacob's tent instead. Apparently in feeling around in the dark and whatever, Jacob doesn't pick up on the switch; he does the deed, and in doing so commits himself to marrying Leah. When Jacob confronts his uncle about the deceit, Laban offers him Rachel too—for seven more years of work.

In the meantime, the two sisters, jealous of each other, engage in a birth-giving contest, the result of which will be twelve sons, each of whom eventually will be the patriarch of one of the twelve tribes of Israel.

When his the seven years of service to Laban is up, Jacob makes ready to leave Laban's household and return to Canaan. But Laban has one more trick up his sleeve, and it leads to a one of the most bizarre instances of divine intervention in all of Scripture. In negotiating his departure Jacob contends that he should be able to take some goats and sheep with him, because Laban's herds were greatly increased under Jacob's care. Jacob proposes to take only ones that are spotted or speckled, because they are less valuable. Laban agrees to this, but then orders his sons to drive all the spotted and speckled animals away, out of Jacob's reach. Thus Jacob is left to tend all the pure-coated animals, none of which he can claim for his own.

This is when Yahweh intercedes. In a dream He reveals to Jacob which of the remaining pure-coated animals have recessive genes for spots and speckles. (31:10) Wow, huh? Using this information Jacob begins a new breeding program and over a six-year period raises a new herd of spotted and speckled animals, fatter and sturdier than Laban's original herd. According to the agreement he made with Laban, they all belong to Jacob.

Of course the story doesn't refer to genes, and mixed in with it are some folk notions about laying peeled branches in watering troughs to encourage mating. But given that Jacob was working with pure-coated animals, and that Yahweh in the dream revealed to him which males would produce spotted or speckled offspring, the editors must have intended for us to understand that Yahweh was giving Jacob inside information about what males would throw spotted animals and which would not, a concept that a nation of herders and farmers surely would understand.

At this point Jacob demands to be released of his obligation to Laban, and the old man reluctantly agrees. Even so, Laban gives half-hearted pursuit as Jacob flees with his wives, his children, and his flocks back to Canaan.

Ambushed by God
Jacob is not that concerned about Laban. He's far more worried about what kind of reception his brother Esau is going to give him. So worried, in fact, that he has a paranoid hallucination in which

he believes he is being attacked by God. This is a stark little epiphany, barely nine lines long, and you either believe it or you don't.

This is the famous wrestling match between Jacob and God. Read as a hallucinogenic experience, it conveys the picture of a man confronting his worst fears the night before a long-dreaded day. Read as the report of an actual event, it's as odd as it is inspiring. As Jacob broods alone by a river, God, in the form of a man, approaches Jacob and without a word begins wrestling with him. When neither gains an upper hand, God attempts to break off the match by striking Jacob's hip and dislocating it. Despite the injury Jacob refuses to let go until he is blessed, and this God grants him, "because you have been strong against God." (32:28) God also gives Jacob a second name, Israel.[2] From this point on the descendents of Jacob will be called "Israelites," and their homeland is called "Israel."

That brings us to the end of Jacob's story. The meeting with Esau goes okay. Everybody's neck hairs are up, but they agree not to fight and Esau goes off to found the kingdom of Edom. Apparently the editors believed that the Edomites play an important role in this story, because the whole of Chapter 36 is devoted to inventorying all the Edomite chiefs who ever lived. Oh *well.* As Shelley's Ozymandius says: "Look on my works, ye Mighty, and despair!" The *Edomites?*

Joseph
Joseph is the Old Testament's first rock star. Not even Moses—the greatest inspirational figure in ancient Hebrew history—arouses

---

[2] The text, for the most part, continues to call him Jacob.

this level of admiration in the Old Testament editors. There is something about a youthful hero outwitting his adversaries that an audience can't resist, and it's this formula the editors use for their two favorite characters, Joseph and David, whom we will be meeting later.

Most everyone remembers from Sunday school the story of Joseph and the Coat of Many Colors. Joseph's father Israel gives young Joseph a splendid coat of many colors (some translations call it a "coat with long sleeves," but it's much more fun to imagine an eye-bending psychedelic garment). Joseph's older brothers, made jealous by this sign of favoritism, jump him, rip off the coat, and throw him down an empty well. After lunch the brothers decide to sell their younger brother to some passing merchants. Realizing they need a cover story, the brothers slaughter a goat and smear Joseph's coat with its blood. Later they show the bloody coat to their distraught father as proof Joseph was killed by a wild animal.

The merchants that bought Joseph travel on to Egypt, where they sell the lad to a member of Pharaoh's court, presumably for a tidy profit. Joseph settles in to his new career as a house slave of a rich man. Unfortunately, he's really good-looking, and the official's wife is smitten. She tries to seduce him, but he quite sensibly demurs. But she doesn't give up, and one day when the house is empty of all but the two of them, she grabs him. He pulls away, leaving his tunic in her hands, which the wife later presents to her husband as proof that Joseph tried to rape her.

 He is thrown in jail. There he gains a reputation as an uncanny interpreter of dreams. Some years later, Pharaoh suffers two nightmares—one about cows and one about corn. When none of his paid staff can explain the dreams to him, the name of the gifted young Israelite inmate comes up.

Joseph interprets Pharaoh's dreams about cows and corn to mean that seven years of famine will follow seven years of plenty. Pharaoh is so impressed by Joseph's calm perspicacity that he makes him governor of all Egypt on the spot.

A gifted administrator, Joseph imposes a tax on Egyptian farmers of one-fifth of their production during the seven years of plenty. When the seven years of famine hits, he's got plenty of surplus grain which he—get this—*sells* back to the Egyptian people. Unbelievable. First he takes their grain as a tax, then he sells it back to them when their hungry.

Of course the demand for grain goes beyond Egypt. The famine is world-wide. News of Egypt's surplus travels fast. Soon families from far and wide are queuing for Joseph's expensive grain.

Family Reunion
One day Joseph sees his brothers in the queue and approaches them. Not recognizing him, the brothers prostrate themselves before him, begging to be allowed to buy food. How more delicious can it get? Joseph decides to have a little fun with them.

First he accuses them of being spies. Practically blubbering, they plead that this is not so. Then Joseph causes money the brothers have spent and objects they did not mean to buy to appear in their sacks, thus making them look like thieves. After a few more stunts like this, the brothers are beside themselves with grief and worry and Joseph finally relents and reveals himself. Word is sent back to Jacob and the rest of the family in Canaan, who prepare to make the journey across the desert. The migration of the Israelites to Egypt is underway.

There is one detail I especially liked. Jacob is worried about the passage to Egypt—he is a very old man and it's going to be a hard journey. Moreover, he is aware that he is leaving the very land that Yahweh supposedly had set aside for his people, and he worries that somehow he is letting Yahweh down. Out of what could only be compassion, Yahweh comes to him in a night vision and assures him that it's all right. "Do not," says Yahweh, "be afraid of going down to Egypt, for I will make you a great nation there. I myself will go down to Egypt with you. I myself will bring you back again...." This puts to rest Jacob's anxiety about pulling out of the Promised Land, but here's the part I liked: "...and Joseph's hand shall close your eyes." (46:4-5) This is one of the few times in the Old Testament where Yahweh treats one of His people with something like love.

Now try to get your mind around this: the migration of *all the Hebrew people in the world* is about to begin. How many people do you think we are we talking about? *Seventy!*

> *The members of the family of Jacob who went to Egypt totaled seventy.*
> 46:27

Later, in *Exodus*, we are given this number again:

> *In all, the descendants of Jacob numbered seventy persons.*
> 1:5-6

It's amazing to think that all of today's Jews—including our Jewish writers, Jewish lawyers, Jewish comics, Jewish directors, Jewish doctors, Jewish mothers—derive from this small band coming in from the desert to Egypt. When they arrive, Pharaoh, prompted by Joseph, welcomes them and basically gives them the land of Goshen in which to settle. That's where *Genesis* ends, not counting a parting flurry of last wishes, blessings, and funerals for Jacob and Joseph.

And as we turn the page and peek at the first few lines of Exodus, we see that the honeymoon of Yahweh and his Chosen People was soon over. By ca. 1300 BCE the Egyptians were once again running Egypt, the capital had been moved back to Thebes, Goshen was a ghetto, and the Israelites were little more than slaves.

In their sorry state, what they needed was a new leader.

Wait, you can hear a baby's cries coming from the reeds down there by the river. Let's send the Pharaoh's daughter to go see what it is…Holy Moses!

The Book of Exodus

It's about 1300 B.C.E now, 400 years after Jacob brought the Israelites in from the desert to settle in Egypt. Joseph's special relationship with Pharaoh is long forgotten. The Israelites are now what they will be for most of their history, a despised and feared minority.

As *Exodus* opens, the new Pharaoh is getting nervous about the size of the Israelite ghetto in Goshen.

> *"Look," he says to his subjects, "these people, these sons of Israel, have become so numerous and strong that they are a threat to us. We must be prudent and take steps against their increasing any further, or if war should break out, they might add to the number of our enemies. They might take arms against us and so escape out of the country."*

1:9-11

He orders a half-hearted genocide in which only the male children were targeted and even then the results were spotty. Moses, for example, survived, and one of the first notable things he does as a youth is to kill an Egyptian supervisor who was beating an Israelite man, and the next day he breaks up a fight between two Israelite men (2:11-14). So apparently there were plenty of male survivors of Pharaoh's edict. Nevertheless, this attempt at genocide is worth noting as the first of many tries throughout history to extinguish this stubborn people.

Everyone who's seen the movie is familiar with how the infant

Moses is saved from the papyrus basket by Pharaoh's daughter and raised as an Egyptian prince, how he got in trouble with the law (for the killing of a cruel Egyptian supervisor, see above) and had to flee to Midian in the out-country, where he marries a pagan woman (who is exceedingly smart, as we shall see later) and settles down to the life of a shepherd.

Yet as content as Moses may have been with that fate, it's not the career Yahweh has in mind for him…

Magic Tricks
It's interesting that Yahweh's first few manifestations in *Exodus* have a kind of homemade quality to them. For example, He announces himself to Moses from within the flames of a burning bush, which is a pretty parlor-level stunt for the Creator of the Universe. Later on He will teach Moses how to change a shepherd's staff into a snake, a trick Pharaoh's own magicians will easily replicate in Chapter 7.

It's hard to avoid the impression that, at this point in His career, Yahweh is not much more than a shabby little desert god trying to muscle His way into the big time. Certainly that is how the other tribes and societies of the time, festooned with their own gods for every occasion, regard Him. They saw the Israelites as a poor people, so it wasn't surprising they only had one God, but that's all He was, just another god. Pharaoh never denies Yahweh's existence, only His authority.

All that is about to change, of course. But first there is a lot of work to do. For the moment, Yahweh is working as Moses' personal coach, trying to bolster his confidence that he can do the job of leading his people out of bondage. It's not easy. Moses readily confesses that he's a painfully shy man, "a slow speaker and not able to speak well." (4:11)

One of the tools Yahweh gives Moses' is a name. ("Yahweh" has been used liberally throughout *Genesis* and up to this moment in *Exodus*, but it actually gets formally introduced here in 3:13.) Biblical Hebrew was written without vowels, and is therefore unpronounceable. The name God gives Moses is rendered as YHWH. The scholars' best guess for how that maye have been pronounced is "Yahweh" (/ˈjaːweɪ/).

Other names—El Shaddai (usually rendered as "God Almighty" and often used in the context of battle), Yahweh Sabboath (also a war name), Elohim (a name favored by Israel's northern tribes that seems to evoke the Holy Ghostian aspect of the divine nimbus)—were available and were used by other contributors to the Old Testament, but there is no doubt that Yahweh is the fundamental name, the name of mystery and power.

"Unaccustomed as I am to public speaking…"
You'd think that being the first human to know God's name as well as the second (since Abraham) to have a back-and-forth conversation with Him would be enough to give Moses plenty of confidence. But it's not. Almost all of Chapter 4 is taken up with Moses' fear of speaking in public. Moses says: "What if they will not believe me or listen to my words and say to me 'Yahweh has not appeared to you'?" The answer is that you enhance your credibility by performing some magic tricks. Yahweh teaches Moses the trick of throwing his staff on the ground to turn it into a snake. Then He shows Moses another one with leprosy sores—first they're there, then they're not! Then another one in which a jug of water turns to blood. With tricks like these, you'd get booed

out of the Poconos. It's no wonder Moses is having a crisis of confidence.

Trying to be tactful, Moses still expresses doubt. "But, my Lord," he says, "never in my life have I been a man of eloquence…"

But Yahweh has had enough of these prevarications. "Now go," he says, "I shall help you to speak and tell you what to say."

Unbelievably, Moses still resists. "[S]end anyone you will!" he begs.

"At this," says the text, "the anger of Yahweh blazed out against Moses…" But then just as quickly Yahweh restrains Himself. With what has to be a deep sigh, He gives in. "There is your brother Aaron the Levite, is there not? I know that he is a good speaker."

Just as Moses is His representative, Yahweh explains, Aaron will be Moses' spokesman. "[H]e will be your mouthpiece," says Yahweh, "and you will be as the god inspiring him."

With this comical negotiation, a friendship of gradually increasing intimacy begins between this shy man and his Maker. This relationship is the psychological bedrock for the rest of the *Exodus* narrative. Moses and his God become a team whose job is to get this perverse, quarrelsome, self-centered people to their Promised Land.

Toward the close of Chapter 4 Yahweh orders Moses to return to Egypt to confront Pharaoh (possibly Ramses II, whose dates—1279-1212 BCE—more or less coincide with the events of *Exodus*). During the journey, however, there is a bizarre incident. Here it is:

> *On the journey, when Moses had halted for the night, Yahweh came to meet him and tried to kill him.*

4:24-25

Say what? No explanation is given for this attack. Only Zipporah, Moses' pagan wife seems to grasp what is going on. Her quick action saves Moses' life:

> *At once Zipporah, taking up a flint, cut off her son's foreskin and with it she touched the genitals of Moses…And Yahweh let him live.*

4:26

Since this is all about genitals, you may imagine Moses' rolling back and forth in the dirt clutching his testicles and screaming with pain as Yahweh grimly crushes them. Moses would have died if Zipporah hadn't figured out what was going on: *Moses had neglected to have his son circumcised!* How could he have forgotten that? The very first thing that Yahweh had commanded Abraham, the patriarch of the Hebrews, to do was to circumcise his people.

So what's the lesson here? First, that Yahweh still isn't very civilized. He's been out alone in the desert a long time. (As we move through the Old Testament, a subtext will be the Israelites' civilizing of their own God.) The second part of the lesson is that Yahweh expects His spokesperson not to be a fool. How could Moses lead the Chosen People out of Egypt if he doesn't even remember the terms of the Second Covenant? Moses himself is circumcised (otherwise Zipporah would have had to fix him up too). But how could he be so *stupid* as to not circumcise his own son?

A Plague Upon You

Now comes the shameful (to lovers of fair play) but action-packed interlude of the ten plagues. First, Moses has to go before Pharaoh and demand he let the Israelites go. Of course Pharaoh refuses. Now the game is on.

Yahweh plays this whole thing like a giant publicity stunt. Apparently He doesn't feel He's attained sufficient status in the eyes of the Egyptians. Pharaoh and his court openly sneer the first time Moses and Aaron (7:8-12) turn a shepherd's staff into a snake. Ha! Even Pharaoh's own magicians can manage that one!

So, one by one, Moses triggers the ten plagues, each one more disturbing than the last:

1. The Egyptians' water supply turns into blood.

2. Frogs rain down from the sky.

3. The dust turns into mosquitoes (this is the desert; there's *lots* of dust).

4. Then come gad flies, also known as horse flies. They bite!

5. All off Egyptians' livestock dies.

6. The Egyptian peoples' skin breaks out in boils

7. A hailstorm crushes uncovered crops and livestock (even though, according to plague #5, all the livestock is dead).

8. A giant swarm of locusts comes to eat up the crops.

9. The land is plunged into total darkness.

After Yahweh administers each plague He gives Pharaoh the chance to relent, but he refuses. But here's the deal: even if Pharaoh wanted to relent and give in, *Yahweh won't let him.* He says so explicitly right at the beginning:

> *I myself will harden his heart, and he will not let the people go.*

4:21

Apparently Yahweh has lost interest in the concept of free will. Remember Adam and Eve? Their most unique quality was that they could choose whether or not to obey God. That's all gone now. Poor Pharaoh is to blame for his intransigence even though he has no control over his own decisions! The whole thing is a Punch and Judy show to convince both the Israelites and the Egyptians that Yahweh is the baddest god of all. In fact, He comes right out and says so Himself! Here's what Moses tells Pharaoh in Yahweh's name:

> *"Had I stretched out my hand to strike you and your subjects with pestilence, you would have been swept from the earth. But I have let you live for this: to have my name published throughout all the earth."*

9:14-17

Poor Pharaoh is nothing more than a sock puppet. It's *so* not fair.

It's interesting to note that the first nine of the ten plagues (chapters 7-11) *could* be associated with a very heavy spring rainy season. The rivers that turn into blood could be thick with red silt. The multitude of frogs could have arisen from the excessive moisture on the ground; the same with the mosquitoes and the gadflies, and even the disease that kills all the livestock. The hail that destroys the crops could be simply a freak spring storm. Quite possibly the locusts (plague number eight) could have benefited from a wet spring, and the ninth plague—three days of darkness—sure sounds like sun-blotting heavy storm clouds. The boils? Maybe it was stress from the first eight plagues.

The tenth plague—the Passover—is another thing entirely. This is the 'I really mean it' plague, the dropping of the atomic bomb, the thunderous rebuttal to Pharaoh's limp-wristed attempt to thin the Israelite population by killing male infants. Yahweh speaks:

> *I will go through the land of Egypt and strike*
> *down all the first-born...man and beast alike,*
> *and I shall deal out punishment to all the gods*
> *of Egypt. I am Yahweh!*

12:12-13

That's the heart of it, but before Yahweh actually strikes the blow there's much preparation to be done. First, the Israelites must mark their dwellings so that the Destroying Angel will know to leave them alone. Patiently, Yahweh instructs Moses and Aaron in the procedure for protecting the Israelites: each family must sacrifice an "unblemished animal," the blood of which is to be daubed over the doorway of the family's home; that night the animal must be roasted and its flesh, "head, feet, and entrails" entirely consumed along with unleavened bread and bitter herbs, not a particle of which is to be left over. Moreover, the meal is to be eaten "hastily," the celebrants fully dressed , as if ready to run at a moment's notice.

The preparations take eight days to carry out. The Destroying Angel is released. The moment is described in chillingly straightforward language:

> *And at midnight Yahweh struck down all the first-born in the land of Egypt: the first-born of Pharaoh, heir to his throne, the first-born of the prisoner in his dungeon, and the first-born of all the cattle. Pharaoh and all his courtiers and all the Egyptians got up in the night, and there was not a house without its dead.*

12:29-31

Today this event, this passing-over of the Destroying Angel and the eight days of preparations leading up to it, are celebrated in the most sacred of Jewish holidays, the Passover.

Naturally the next morning Pharaoh invited the Israelites to depart Egypt—*now, for Godsake!* Good thing the people were ready. The closing verses of Chapter 12 note that they now numbered about 600,000 people (quite a nice return on the original seventy) and had resided in Egypt for 430 years.

Put on Your 3-D Glasses
Of all the books of the Old Testament, *Exodus* probably had the largest special-effects budget. (*Revelation* takes the overall prize. But that's in New Testament.) In much the same way as Shakespeare inserted characters and scenes into his plays to keep the less well-read members of the audience entertained, so the editors of the Old Testament sprinkle their narrative with jaw-dropping and sometimes gratuitous tales of adventure, slaughter, and heroism, to keep childish listeners from losing interest.

None is more gratuitous than the anticlimactic episode of Moses parting the Sea of Reeds to provide an escape route from the pursuing Egyptians. Yes, the Sea of Reeds, *not* the Red Sea named by older translations, whose parting truly would have been an accomplishment of, well, Biblical proportions. As its name implies, the Sea of Reeds was probably a seasonal bog, knee to waist-deep all the way across. In any case, Yahweh manages to dry up the Sea of Reeds overnight "with a strong easterly wind," (14:22) enough that, at least, it could be traversed by the Israelites on foot. But not by the Egyptians on chariot.

> *[Yahweh] so clogged their chariot wheels that*
> *they could scarcely make headway.*

14:25

This episode by the Sea of Reeds consumes most of two chapters (14 & 15), and yet does not advance the narrative one iota—on the far side of the Sea of Reeds the Chosen People are still the same bewildered, muttering mob they were on the Egyptian side. Yet this episode is one of the most widely-remembered of all the Old Testament adventures.

Getting to Know You
Now that Yahweh has escaped with his Chosen People into the desert, the hard work of building a relationship begins. In some respects they are like a newly-eloped couple. Finally, alone at last, still panting from the exertions of emancipation, they really look at each other for the first time: Yahweh, sputtering, dusty, fiery and dangerous, an as-yet uncivilized desert god with the chutzpah to think He can muscle in and compete with established deities like Baal; and the ingénue-Israelites, feeling suddenly uncertain and vulnerable, like a girl in a desert motel with her bearded biker lover.

Yahweh, to give him the benefit of the doubt, must have envisioned this period as a sort of shakedown cruise. He had already assessed the Israelites (13:17) as not yet ready for the task of conquering Palestine. So apparently the idea was to undertake a little basic training out here in the desert, preparing the people for the battle ahead. Of course, with His omniscience, He must have known how arduous this training phase was really going to be. (See *Doing Hard Time* below.) For now, however, we're still honeymooning, hopes fairly high.

Yahweh and Moses set up a system for food and water. For water Moses merely raps on a rock with his staff, creating a stream; food arrives in the form of daily downpours of fresh quail, followed by a dew-like precipitation of manna ("…like coriander seed; it was white and its taste was like that of wafers made with honey" [16:31]). Then Moses and his advisors begin to work out a system for self-government. By now (Chapter 19) the Israelites have set up a semi-permanent camp at the base of Mount Sinai. Yahweh has stationed Himself on the mountaintop. Moses, adapting to the role of intermediary between God and his people, becomes history's first shuttle diplomat, trekking regularly up the mountain with the people's demands and concerns and returning with Yahweh's pronouncements.

The Ten Commandments and the New Covenant
The background noise for this section is grumbling and mistrust on the part of the Chosen People, who complain about every campsite and whine about every meal. This ingratitude is a constant source of irritation for Yahweh, who can't help but wonder why by now He hasn't earned a modicum of unconditional faith. As in any good story, this tension continues to build, with the promise of an eruption to come.

Meanwhile, it's time to prepare a contract and have it notarized by a fiery finger. Yahweh actually makes a date three days hence to manifest Himself before his people, and as with any first date everyone seems appropriately nervous. The people wash their clothes, and Moses commands the men to "not go near any woman." (19:15)

For all that, however, it doesn't go well. Unfortunately, Yahweh comes on a little too strong and scares the bejeezus out of His people. For starters, He wraps Mount Sinai in a cloud and descends onto it in the form of fire, accompanied by lightning flashes. Deafening celestial trumpets sound and Yahweh Himself speaks as peals of thunder. He repeatedly warns everyone not to come too close to the mountain or they will die. By now everyone is peeing on their sandals. After a few minutes of this the people come to Moses:

> *"Speak to us yourself," they said to Moses,*
> *"and we will listen; but do not let God speak to*
> *us, or we shall die."*

20:19-20

And with that, the priesthood is invented. Ordinary people can no longer speak with God.

But Yahweh's first face-to-face meeting with His people isn't a complete disaster. Before the Israelites are completely overcome with fear He does manage to thunder out the Ten Commandments.

You'd think that would be enough. But this is Yahweh, after all, the Israelite God, a stickler for details. He wants to draw up a new covenant. Calling Moses and Aaron up to the mountain to meet with Him, the three of them put their heads together to go over the fine print.

We won't rehash the whole massive contract, but the level of detail is at times quite amazing. For example, Yahweh bans altars with steps (along with altars made of dressed stones or constructed with tools of any kind [20:24-26]) because in climbing up the steps the priest might accidentally expose himself to those worshipping below. Yech! I'm sure everybody agreed with that one.

There's a section on slave management, one on fighting, even one on animal control, all directly from Yahweh's mouth:

> *"When an ox gores a man or woman to death, the ox must be stoned. Its flesh shall not be eaten, and the owner of the ox shall not be liable. But if the ox has been in the habit of goring before, and if its owner was warned but has not kept it under control, then should this ox kill a man or woman, the ox must be stoned and its owner put to death."*

21:28-30

Glad we got *that* cleared up! Another is a shepherds-beware type of warning:

> *"Anyone who has intercourse with an animal must die."*

22:19

And:

> *"You must not boil a kid in its mother's milk."*

23:19

(Gad! People did that?)

And a bit of history retrospectively presented as prophecy:

> *"...I shall make all your enemies turn and run from you...* [But, and a big but it is] *I shall not drive them out before you in a single year, or the land would become a desert where, to your cost, the wild beasts would multiply. Little by little I will drive them out before you until your numbers grow and you come into possession of the land."*[3]

23:27-31

Having dictated all this, Yahweh instructs Moses to bring up a group of selected elders to approach Him directly—but still at a safe distance.

> *Moses went up with Aaron, Nadab and Abihu, and seventy elders of Israel. They saw the God of Israel beneath whose feet there was, it seemed, a sapphire pavement pure as the heavens themselves. He laid no hand on these notables of the sons of Israel; they gazed on God. They ate and they drank.*

24:9-11

This is the last time in the Bible that ordinary men are allowed in the presence of God.

---

[3] In other words, the editors, working from the hindsight of history, had to concede that in fact the Israelites acquired their Promised Land on the installment plan. But see, that's the way Yahweh *planned* it.

Apparently, the pre-nup is still in rough draft form (the later version of the Ten Commandments, for example, will exclude the threats of everlasting vengeance that spice up the first draft). Yahweh orders Moses to spend the next forty days and nights with Him on the mountain inscribing the final draft on stone tablets, as well as working out the details of a host of other issues, such as the construction of the portable tabernacle that will house the Ark of the Covenant. This is not a wish list, nor even a description of the elements of Yahweh's entourage. These are *plans*, detailed enough that the tabernacle, the altars, and the vestments could be fashioned from these passages alone. Listen to this description of the robe the high priest Aaron must wear whenever he enters the sanctuary housing Yahweh. The level of detail is astonishing:

> *You are to make the robe of the ephod entirely of violet-purple. In the center it must have an opening for the head, the opening to have around it a border woven like the neck of a coat of mail to keep the robe from being torn. The lower hem you are to decorate with pomegranates of purple stuffs, violet shade and red, crimson stuffs, and fine twined linen, with golden bells between: gold bells and pomegranates alternately all around the lower hem of the robe. Aaron is to wear it when he officiates, so that the tinkling of the bells will be heard whenever he enters the sanctuary into Yahweh's presence, or leaves it; thus he will not die.*

28:31-35

Don't forget the bells, whatever you do.

Toga Party

Of course forty days is a long time. The tens of thousands of ordinary Israelites waiting in the desert below are getting more restless by the day, worried that they've been abandoned.

Coming to Aaron, they demand that he fashion a good old pagan deity—a golden calf—to rule them in Moses' and Yahweh's absence. This seemingly-gratuitous lapse of faith is actually a continuing theme between the Chosen People and their God. As high-minded as Yahweh is, His eye ever fixed on Eternity, throughout the Old Testament He tends to be inattentive to day-to-day matters that the pagan gods are very good at—fertility issues, harvest blessings, weather control. When Yahweh is unresponsive to the people's need for help in quotidian matters, they turn to other gods. This is a conflict that will come to a head in *Samuel I* and *II*.

The immediate problem, however, is the golden calf; Yahweh is furious about it. He makes ready to destroy all these ungrateful Israelites and start over again: "I can see how headstrong these people are!" Yahweh says to Moses. "Leave me now, my wrath shall blaze out against them and devour them." (32:10)

Here's where Moses shows his true gift, which is his ability to placate the feelings of the Lord God of the Universe and bring Him around to another way of thinking. He appeals to Yahweh's sense of justice and fidelity to prior commitments:

> *Remember Abraham, Isaac and Jacob, your*
> *servants to whom by your own self you swore*
> *and made this promise: I will make your*
> *offspring as many as the stars of heaven, and*
> *all the land which I promised I will give to your*

> *descendants, and it shall be their heritage forever.*

32:13-14

Does Yahweh want to be seen as a God who breaks His word? Above all, however, Moses appeals to Yahweh's vanity:

> *Why should the Egyptians say, 'It was with evil intent that he brought them out, to kill them in the mountains and to wipe them off the face of the earth'? Turn from your fierce anger; relent and do not bring disaster on your people.*

32:12

'He's got a point,' you can hear Yahweh thinking.

"So Yahweh relented," concludes the text. But Moses does not. As soon as he wins the argument he assumes for himself the anger that Yahweh has just relinquished. He shatters the tablets—forty days worth of close legal writing—at the foot of the mountain. With Aaron standing nearby, wringing his hands and trying to avoid blame ("You know yourself," he whines to Moses, "how prone this people is to evil." 32:23) Moses grinds the golden calf into powder and scatters it on the water, "…and he made the sons of Israel drink it."

Then Moses positions himself at the gate of the camp and roars, "'Who is for Yahweh? To me!' And all the sons of Levi rallied to him." (32:26) Moses leads this little force forward to slaughter some three thousand of the worst golden calf offenders, which one supposes, is better than Yahweh's plan of wiping out the whole encampment. For their act of loyalty, the Levites will get a monopoly on the priesthood.

Yahweh, however, is still upset. Almost wearily he tells Moses to resume the journey to the Promised Land, but adds that He Himself will not be accompanying them, because he is still angry enough at this "headstrong people" that He might exterminate them on the way. (33:1-5)

Once again Moses rises up to dissuade Him. It is extraordinary, the status this shy man has gained with his God since that night in the desert when Yahweh silently tried to kill him. Here's Moses' plea:

> *Remember…that this nation is your own people.… If you are not going with us yourself, do not make us leave this place. By what means can it be known that I, I and my people, have won your favor, if not by your going with us?*

33:12-17

Yahweh, touched, relents.

Think of it: twice in one day Moses has succeeded in changing Yahweh's mind! Slowly but surely Yahweh is coming to understand that the raised fist and the heavy hand are not the way to go with this people. Before our eyes Moses is helping to civilize his own God.

In this glowing moment, Moses tries for something even more extraordinary: a peek at Yahweh's living face! At first the Deity kindly demurs, explaining that a "man cannot see me and live." Yet like the good partners they have become, they fashion a compromise: Yahweh will shield Moses with His hand as the rest of His Ineffable Substance passes by. "…you shall see the back of me, but my face is not to be seen," warns Yahweh (33:23), and so it is done, though the text is silent on just what God's backside looks like.

Now it's time to set out for the Promised Land.

The Book of Leviticus

From the point-of-view of narrative construction the editors have us right where they want us, on the cusp of the Great Adventure of the Israelites heading out for the Promised Land. As readers, we're dying to get on with the story. We'll put up with almost anything to find out what happens next.

What happens next is *Leviticus*. Really? Yes, before we get on with the story, we have to sort through the droning body of laws that outline what it takes to be a good Israelite.

The Men's Club
In *Leviticus* we begin to see clearly what we've known all along: the Bible was written for men. Women hardly exist in the Old Testament except as a source of uncleanness, temptation, and wrong thinking. Here, as Yahweh spells out the rules (remember He's speaking every word in real time), the women of the community are allowed to listen in as the men receive the laws. What the women learn is that, from the point-of-view of the men, they're the source of many of the problems that men have to protect themselves from.

I see no reason to put the reader through a verse-by-verse gloss of this material. A survey of some of the high points will give you a feel for how obsessively detailed these laws are:

Section One is called "The Ritual of Sacrifice," describing the four main types of sacrifice: Communion Sacrifice, Sacrifice for Sin, Sacrifice of Reparation, and Sacrifice for the Investiture of

Priests. All involve major butchering of many animals—bulls and rams and oxen.

Section Two is "The Investiture of the Priests," describing a ceremony of huge pomp and circumstance punctuated by ten ritual sacrifices that constitute the ordination of Aaron and his sons as once-and-future priests of Yahweh.

Section Three covers "Rules Concerning the Clean and the Unclean." The level of detail here is astonishing. Here is the passage on winged insects:

> *All winged insects that move on four[4] feet you must hold detestable. Of all these winged insects you may eat only the following: those that have legs above their feet so that they can leap over the ground. These are the ones you may eat: the several kinds of migratory locust, solham, hargol and hagab locusts in their several kinds. But all winged insects on four feet you are to hold detestable.*
> 11:20-23

There are subsections for creatures that live in water, birds (among which bats are listed; zoology wasn't Yahweh's strongest subject), hoofed animals, and "small ground beasts:"

> *Any small beast that crawls on the ground is*

---

[4] You will notice that Aristotle's notion of actually observing the natural world—to notice, for example that insects have *six* legs—has not yet made its appearance in the Jewish history of ideas. Here the writer is probably trying to distinguish between insects that crawl—detestable!—and winged insects that hop around.

> *detestable; you must not eat it. Anything that moves on its belly, anything that moves on four legs or more—in short all the small beasts that crawl on the ground—you must not eat these because they are detestable.*
>
> 11:41-43

Snakes and lizards, I guess.

Don't Touch Me There
Now we move on to Chapter 15, the sexual impurities of men and women. The text in 15:3 provides the basic directive: "When a man has a discharge from his body," [a symptom of venereal disease] he should be isolated from all social contact. Even after he is cured, "he must allow seven days for his purification." (15:13) But if the discharge is a simple ejaculation (achieved by what means the text studiously ignores) he is only unclean until evening. (15:16)

For women, it's more complicated. There is, above all, the horror of menstruation. The strategy for avoiding having to deal with it requires that men refrain from the company of women at least fourteen days out of the month. (The prescribed time for menstruation is seven days, and though this can be extended it cannot be shortened. Then the woman needs an additional seven days to purify herself.)

The depth of male revulsion about all this is breathtaking. When a woman is menstruating,

> *Any bed she lies on in this state will be unclean; any seat she sits on will be unclean.*

> *Anyone who touches her bed must wash his clothing and wash himself and will be unclean until evening.*
>
> *Anyone who touches any seat she has sat on must wash his clothing and wash himself and will be unclean until evening. If there is anything on the bed or the chair on which she sat, anyone who touches it will be unclean until evening.*

15:19-23

If a man should sleep with her during this time, he will be unclean for seven days. That's surprisingly mild, as Old Testament castigations go; one senses the smirk of forbearance. Consider that you're unclean (must remove yourself from contact with the community) until evening even if you have sex *according* to the rules!

Leprosy

The longest subsection under "Rules Concerning the Clean and Unclean" is about leprosy, the most feared of Biblical diseases. The text here sheds its scolding tone and simply lays out the facts in clinical fashion and suggests practical forms of diagnosis. The only known treatment was isolation.

> *A man infected with leprosy must wear his clothing torn and his hair disordered; he must shield his upper lip and cry, "Unclean, unclean." As long as the disease lasts he must be unclean; and therefore he must live apart: he must live outside the camp.*

13:45-46

There is an odd exception to this edict.

> *"But if the leprosy spreads all through the skin, if it covers him entirely from head to foot so far as the priest can see, then the priest must examine the sick person and, if he finds that the leprosy covers his whole body, declare the sick person clean. But as soon as an ulcer appears on him, he will be unclean.*

13:12-15

Today, people with leprosy (now known as Hansen's disease), if properly treated with antibiotics, can mingle with non-infected people. Modern treatment is not always available, however. In many countries, isolation remains the preferred mode of treatment. In India alone there are still more than one thousand leper colonies. There is even an active leper colony in the U.S., on the Hawaiian island of Molokai.

The Scapegoat

Being a scapegoat is not just a fate reserved for defeated politicians. *Leviticus 16* describes the annual ceremony of the Day of Atonement, the main feature of which is the preparation of two goats, one for Yahweh and one for Azazel, a demon of the desert. The goat for Yahweh is slaughtered in the usual fashion. But as for the goat for Azazel:

> *Aaron must lay his hands on its head and confess all the faults of the sons of Israel, all their transgressions and all their sins, and lay them to its charge. Having thus laid them on the goat's head, he shall send it out into the desert led by a man waiting ready, and the goat*

> *will bear all their faults away with it into a desert place.*
> 16:21-22

Afterwards, everyone goes home, feeling much, much better.

Section Four, which takes up the rest of *Leviticus,* is "The Law of Holiness" which describes in excruciating detail the social mores of observant Israelites, including nakedness (practically always forbidden), homosexuality ("hateful"), and bestiality ("foul"). You are also not allowed to wear a garment made from two different kinds of fabric (19:19), nor are you "to round off your hair at the edges nor trim the edges of your beard…and you are not to tattoo yourselves." (19:27-28) This section also includes the famous "eye for eye, tooth for tooth" utterance (24:19-22) that everyone associates the Old Testament with. It's called the Law of Retaliation.

Ghetto Economy

Given the torrent of bizarre details in *Leviticus* it's easy to lose sight of the underlying purpose—to unite and hold firm the Jewish community living in exile in a Babylonian ghetto in the late sixth century BCE

Aside from the rules governing worship, food, sexual and social relations, the priests came up with an additional web of regulations governing *economic* relationships, some of which remain with us to this day, though in much changed form.

Based upon the model of the six days it took Yahweh to create the universe, with the seventh for rest, the priests broke everything down into sevenths—$6/7^{ths}$ of work for every $1/7^{th}$ of rest. You can work your fields for six years, for example, but in the seventh year they must rest.

Then there is the Year of the Jubilee. It comes once every 50 years (the year after seven times seven). In the Year of the Jubilee all debts are cancelled and all property is returned to the original owner. "Land," says Yahweh, "must not be sold in perpetuity, for the land belongs to me, and to me you are only strangers and guests." (25:23-24). Also, during the Year of Jubilee almost no work is done. "...you will not sow, you will not harvest..., you will not gather..." (25:11-12), and all slaves are freed. (26:54) No wonder our word "jubilation" means wild joy; in Spanish, "jubilación" is the word for retirement.

There are, however, some subtleties buried within the rules for the Year of Jubilee that Yahweh hastens to point out to His people:

> *If you buy from your neighbor, this must take into account the number of years since the [last] jubilee; according to the number of productive years will he fix the price. The greater the number of years, the higher shall be the price demanded; the less the number of years, the greater the reduction; for what he is selling you is a certain number of harvests.*
> 25:15-17

That's pretty shrewd advice Yahweh is offering to potential buyers. He's saying that the value of property decreases the closer you are to the Year of Jubilee. In year one of the fifty-year span the property is worth a certain amount. In year twenty-five it is worth half of that. In year forty-nine it is worth almost nothing.

How to Calculate the Gratuity

Finally, now that the priesthood is a full-time profession, there has to be a way for priests to make a living. The solution? They are allowed to keep portions of the offerings they make to Yahweh on behalf of the community. The rules are summarized in 10:12-15. If the offering is one of flour (an oblation) the priests mix it with oil and incense (but never leavening), burn some of it on the altar (Yahweh's portion) and cook the rest on a griddle for themselves. If the offering is a sacrifice of an animal, the priests may keep the breast and right thigh (7:28-34).

That solves the problem of food, but priests need some disposable income as well, wouldn't you think? Here's how that works. Every person in the community is assigned a value: "…a man between 20 and 50 years of age shall be valued at 50 silver shekels…a woman shall be valued at 30 shekels…" (27:3-4) and so on, with differing values assigned to boys and girls, children, and senior citizens. Anyone who wants to consecrate him- or herself to Yahweh in order to receive a blessing knows exactly how much to place in the tip basket.

Another good source of income for the priesthood is the 20% rule, which is the standard penalty for failing somehow to make a proper offering, a transgression that only the priests are qualified to pass judgment on. That's 20% *in cash*, thank you very much. Even if you change your mind and decided not to make an offering today, the priests still get their 20%. In addition, the priests have the right to all first-born animals plus every tenth one after that. (See Chapter 27, Tariffs and Estimates.)

If you were inclined to be cynical about such things, you might believe that someone of the priestly persuasion was the real author of this stuff.

Now onto the next book, *Numbers*. We'll skip over the first ten chapters (more priestly rules) and get on with the real adventure, the march to Canaan. (Traveler's tip: bring an extra pair of sandals; this is going to take a while—forty years, to be exact.)

The Book of Numbers

The Book of Numbers starts out trying to be exactly what its title implies—a census of Israelite men over the age of twenty who would be available for military service. The total for all the families (minus the Levites—fighting priests haven't been invented yet) is 603,550. It's a big number, one that scholars find hard to credit, but it's arrived at in a very precise manner, clan by clan, so you have to lend it some credibility.

However, the real subject of *Numbers* is not arithmetic but the journey through the wilderness to the Promised Land. Before we get to that, however, the priests get in one more egregious jab at women. It's called the Oblation for Jealousy (5:11-31). Basically it requires that any woman who has aroused the jealousy of her husband, whether unjustly or not, must undergo a literally gut-wrenching ritual in order to cleanse the poor man of his ill feeling. After a round of ceremonial offerings, imprecations and purifications, she is required to drink water into which dirt from the tabernacle floor has been stirred. This is the floor where all the sacrifices take place; it would be like drinking tea made from the sweepings of a butcher shop. If the woman gets sick, she's guilty; if she doesn't, she's innocent. In either case, "The husband shall be guiltless, but the woman must bear the punishment for her sin." Where is Susan B. Anthony when you need her?

With that taken care of, the adventure can begin in earnest.

"If you kids don't shut up…"
From the very outset of their journey the Israelites start misbehaving like children in the back of a minivan, with Yahweh overreacting like an exasperated parent at the wheel. It's hard to

find pages in the Bible more packed with ill-temper and hurt feelings than chapters 11 through 17 of *Numbers*.

The troubles start three days into the journey. The Israelites start complaining about the food:

> *"Who will give us meat to eat?" they said.*
> *"Think of the fish we used to eat free in Egypt,*
> *the cucumbers, melons, leeks, onions and*
> *garlic! Here we are wasting away, stripped of*
> *everything; there is nothing but manna for us to*
> *look at!"*

11:5-6

'Sick of manna, are you? You want meat to eat?' replies an enraged Yahweh. 'Coming up!' (11:18) and He stirs up a wind that redirects a flock of quail to the camp. Apparently some of the people are wary about the windfall, knowing how angry their God is, and they are the smart ones. The others—the greedy ones, the loudest complainers—have a fine time preparing these little gifts from God. After they have cooked up their quail and begun to eat,

> *The meat was still between their teeth, not even*
> *chewed, when the anger of Yahweh blazed out*
> *against the people. Yahweh struck them with a*
> *very great plague.*

11:33

Lethal food poisoning, the first step in Yahweh's plan to start weeding out the weaklings whose faith in Him has wavered.

The crisis over the lack of meat is not the only conflict. Moses complains bitterly to Yahweh about his workload:

> *I am not able to carry this nation by myself alone; the weight is too much for me. If this is how You want to deal with me, I would rather You killed me!*

11:14-15

Wouldn't you think such petulance would earn a raised hand from this short-tempered God? Not with Moses, the teacher's pet. At this stage in the journey, Moses can do no wrong in Yahweh's eyes. Arrangements are quickly made to delegate some of Moses' responsibilities among seventy elders.

No sooner is that taken care of than Aaron and Miriam (Moses' sister) denounce Moses for having married a Cushite woman (Zipporah, the clever girl whose quick-thinking saved Moses' life when Yahweh tried to kill him in *Exodus* 4:24). They should have known better than to speak out against Moses. For their impertinence, Yahweh turns Miriam into a leper, with Aaron blubbering for mercy, which is granted (as usual, nothing happens to the man). With Moses interceding for her, Yahweh agrees to reduce Miriam's punishment to a simple one-week banishment; not much worse than being sentenced to the red tent for having a menstrual period.

All this in less than five days on the road. Chosen People or not, here, at the outset of their great adventure, this was by no means a unified community. The danger of this kind of disarray is obviously something the editors wanted to impress upon their Jewish readers. Throughout most of their history Jews have been threatened with extinction. Banding and bonding together as a single people is their best defense.

"We felt like grasshoppers"

The troubles continue. At Yahweh's urging, Moses organizes a party of young men "to reconnoiter the land of Canaan." (13:17) Though on their return all of the scouts agree that Canaan is a beautiful land flowing with milk and honey, some of the group warn that it is inhabited by dangerous giants[5] who live in large fortified towns. "We felt like grasshoppers, and so we seemed to them." (13:33)

> *At this, the whole community raised their voices and cried aloud, and the people wailed all that night.*

14:1-2

Yahweh's disgust knows no bounds:

> *"How long will this people insult Me? How long will they refuse to believe in Me despite the signs I have worked among them? I will strike them with a pestilence and disown them."*

14:11-12

Forty Years in the Desert
As Yahweh prepares to wipe this impossible race from the face of the earth, Moses intervenes. By now it's clear that his primary job is to talk Yahweh down from these murderous tantrums, and once again he succeeds brilliantly.

His argument is that if Yahweh commits genocide against His own people it will make Him look bad. The skeptics of other nations,

---

[5] The Hebrew word used here is "nephilim," whom we last encountered in *Genesis 6:4*. They are the offspring of the mating of angels with human women.

> *...will say, 'Yahweh was not able to bring this people into the land He swore to give them, and so He has slaughtered them in the wilderness.' No, my Lord! It is now you must display Your power, according to those words You spoke.*

14:16-17

Yahweh sees the sense of this and withdraws His threat. But He insists that some punishment is in order, and this is what He decides: no one currently in the company will live to see the Promised Land.

> *"As for you* [faithless ones]*, your dead bodies will fall in this wilderness, and your sons will be nomads in the wilderness for forty years, bearing the weight of your faithlessness, until the last of you lies dead in the desert."*

14:32-34

And with that Yahweh strikes dead all the members of the scouting party (save two, Caleb and Joshua, who dissented from the majority report). All in all, not a good start for the fabled journey to the Promised Land. And the troubles aren't not over yet.

The Rebellion of the Priests

The most serious uprising occurs in chapters 16 and 17, when a man named Korah, part of the priestly community of the Levites, leads a group of 250 elders that take issue with Moses' and Aaron's exalted position within the community.

> *"You take too much on yourselves! The whole community and all its members are consecrated, and Yahweh lives among them.*

> *Why set yourselves higher than the community of Yahweh?"*

16:3

These are serious issues. If they're all Chosen People, how can Moses and Aaron be more chosen than the rest of them? These dissenters want good, sensible reasons why they should follow Moses' and Aaron's orders. They don't doubt that Yahweh is a powerful god, but here they reveal that they do doubt that He knows what He's doing. Is it really necessary that they wander interminably in the desert as impoverished nomads just because Yahweh says so?

> *"Was it not enough to take us from a land where milk and honey flow to die in this wilderness, without seeking to lord it over us now?... Do you expect this people to be blind?*

16:13-15

Tested beyond endurance, Yahweh again prepares to strike them all down at once, but Moses and Aaron beg him to hold His hand. Needing to punish *somebody*, Yahweh tells Moses to warn everyone to stand clear of the dwellings of Korah, leader of this rebellion, and of Dathan and Abiram, his main supporters. The crowd of onlookers draws away from these suddenly dangerous neighbors. In a poignant detail, the three men are described as "standing at their tent doors, with their wives and their sons and their young children." (16:28) That's when "the ground split open under their feet...and swallowed them, their families too..." (16:32)[6] For good measure, Yahweh vaporizes the 250 supporters

---

[6] The passage goes on to say that they "went down alive to Sheol," the pre-Christian afterworld to which all the dead were consigned, saints and sinners

of the rebellion as well.

You'd think that would settle it, but instead it gets much, much worse: "On the following day the entire community...grumbled against Moses and Aaron." (17:6) What is going on here? Why can't Yahweh silence the complaints? Yahweh, His ire once again aroused, sends down plague to kill them all. Once *again* Moses saves the day, performing an emergency rite of atonement. Only 14,700 Israelites succumbed to the plague before Moses interceded.

This chronic problem of the people losing faith in Yahweh, and Yahweh losing interest in protecting them, will continue to threaten their commitment to one another throughout the Old Testament.

Basic Combat Training

As a newly-hatched and still disorganized community, the Israelites are nearly defenseless out there in the desert. None of the established kingdoms in the area—the Midianites, the Amalekites, the Edomites, the Moabites, and especially the targeted Canaanites—is about to let them settle in and start claiming land.

For the time being they must resign themselves to being nomads. The truth is that none of this is going to improve until the Israelites learn to fight for themselves. They need to develop and train warriors that can be mustered into a standing army, and that's going to take time; about, say, forty years.

---

alike. Though the Old Testament lays the poetic basis for more flamboyant ideas about life after death, Heaven and Hell as such won't be invented until the New Testament.

Chapters 20 through 22 give us a fast-forward of the Israelites' development as a fighting force. At first, like a new kid at school, the Israelites are easy pickings for bullies like the Edomites (descendents of Esau, Jacob's brother), who refuse the wanderers permission even to pass through their lands. But one day the group stands up to one of them, the king of Arad, and "laid them under the ban." (This phrase, which is used often in the Old Testament, is a kind of stern euphemism for slaughtering everyone in the enemy camp—men, women, and children.) After that the reputation of the Israelites as a new force in the desert begins to grow.

Moses and Aaron Offend Yahweh
Just as things are about to look up for the Israelites, Moses, with Aaron's complicity, manages to offend Yahweh so deeply that Yahweh removes them as leaders of the people and prohibits them both from ever setting foot in the Promised Land.

Exactly what they did to deserve this is not clear. Sometimes myths, and legends, and folk histories filter down to us with important parts missing. Apparently the offense (20:6-13) occurred during one of the water crises, with the people wailing and grumbling about being thirsty. Yahweh commands Moses to produce water from a rock, just as he did in *Exodus* 17. But something in the way he does it this time offends Yahweh. It's probably that he doesn't give Yahweh full credit for performing the miracle. Instead, he and Aaron stand before the people and Moses says:

> *"Listen now, you rebels. Shall we make water*
> *gush from this rock for you?"*
20:10-11

Not "Shall Yahweh…" but "Shall *we*.…" Oops.

The punishment is clear enough, however. Poor Aaron is drummed out of the priesthood like a disgraced soldier being stripped of his commission.

> *In the sight of the whole community they went up Mount Hor. Moses stripped Aaron of his garments and put them on Eleazar his son; and Aaron died there on top of the mountain.*
20:28

Moses' punishment will be postponed for some time, so that he can fulfill his duty to shepherd the people to the Promised Land. But he knows that he's no longer the teacher's pet.

Balaam—Have Curse, Will Travel
Out on the battlefront the Israelite military victories continue to mount, and their reputation as a fighting force grows to the point that kings are terrified to learn even that they're approaching. They are now "a horde now cropping everything around us as an ox crops the grass of the fields," laments Balak, King of Moab. (22:4)

In fact, so frightened is this king that he hires the legendary sorcerer Balaam, to help neutralize the supernatural powers of the Israelite god. The Balaam episode reads like an old folktale woven into the dry narrative of *Numbers* in order to jazz up the story and highlight the fact that the Israelites have reached a critical threshold in their history.

King Balak summons Balaam, with the enticement of a generous fee for his services. But Yahweh (probably consulted through the sorcerer's divinations) orders him to refuse. Again the king solicits Balaam's help, sweetening the deal, and this time Balaam accepts. But as soon as he sets out to meet with the king Yahweh sends a destroying angel after him.

And here we have the unmistakable elements of a folk tale, for though Balaam cannot see the angel standing in the road ready to destroy him, sword in hand, his donkey does see the apparition and quite rightly refuses to proceed. Three times the donkey balks at going forward, and three times Balaam beats the animal. Suddenly the donkey begins to complain in fluent Hebrew: "Why beat me three times like this?... Am I not your donkey, and have I not been your mount from your youth? In all this time, have I ever failed to serve you?" (22:29-30) At that moment the Balaam's eyes open and he sees the angel, who, after reprimanding him for beating his donkey, unaccountably gives Balaam permission to continue his journey. The narrative intention seems to be to make Balaam aware that Yahweh was going to be very close by during his dealings with King Balak.

Three times King Balak prepares, at Balaam's direction, elaborate altars for the sorcerer to perform the ritual of cursing the king's enemies, and three times Yahweh returns the answer, 'These people will not be conquered; you will be conquered by them.' And with that Balaam goes home.

Understandably intimidated and demoralized, King Balak refrains from attacking. And surprisingly, the Israelites do the same. Instead, they set up a permanent camp on the Moabite plains (just east of Jerusalem), and the two peoples appear to settle into a peaceful co-existence. One gets the impression that many of the forty years of the so-called "wandering" pass here in this peaceful interlude.

Those Midianite Girls
But here is—at least from the Old Testament point-of-view—where the sinister Balaam really earns his money. On his advice (31:16), the Moabites, the Midianites and the other Baal-worshipping tribes begin to intermarry with the Israelites. (Don't forget that Moses took a Midianite wife for himself, back at the beginning of his career.) You can practically hear Balaam rubbing his hands and chortling as the "people gave themselves over to debauchery with the daughters of Moab." (25:1-2)

In the ensuing crisis, Yahweh tries to annihilate his own people once again. He looses one of His fast-acting plagues, but just in time Phinehas, son of the new high priest Eleazar, seizes a lance and runs a rutting miscegenating couple "right through the groin," (25:8) which appeases Yahweh's rage. The plague disappears after killing only 24,000 people, which, more or less coincidentally, finishes off the last of the older generation that had been sentenced to wander in the desert until they died, thus clearing the way for their children to push on to the Promised Land.

This sweeping away of the older generation includes even Moses, whom Yahweh gently reminds will not be allowed to set foot in Canaan. Don't shed a tear for him just yet, though. He will take longer to shuffle off the stage than Jimmy Durante. His farewell exhortation will consume the whole of *Deuteronomy*.

Dividing the Spoils
Meantime, there are more rules to announce. Now that the Chosen People are about to move into their new homeland and can anticipate a big increase in their quality of life, Yahweh suddenly finds Himself in need of more burnt offerings. He has 23,000 priests and their households to feed, after all, none of whom are required to do any productive work except kosher butchering. The

updated list of required offerings goes on for two pages: thousands of lambs, rams, and bulls; tons of bread and flour; many hins (about a gallon) of wine; and of course, one scapegoat to pack off into the desert with all the community's sins.

Supremely confident of their ability to conquer Canaan, the leaders of the twelve Israelite tribes hold a pre-campaign meeting to decide how the land will be divided among them. Here (in Chapter 32) the tribes of Reuben and Gad and the eastern half of the tribe of Manasseh spring a surprise: they no longer want to be part of the deal. Cattle and sheep herders, they like the broad Moabite lands where they've been living for years. Moses reluctantly approves their plan, as long as they agree to fight alongside the rest of the Israelites in the campaign to take Canaan.

Then he takes a very deep breath, and what follows is *The Book of Deuteronomy.*

The Book of Deuteronomy

Deuteronomy is the parliamentarian of the Pentateuch. After all the clamor, squabbling, bloodletting and primitive adventures of the first four books, a pomaded and grave *Deuteronomy* stands up to enunciate what it's all supposed to mean. Supposedly the transcript of Moses' final three sermons, it is in effect a commencement speech to the Israelites on graduating from the desert. Even as Moses speaks they are gathering arms and making other preparations for the thrust into Canaan. Like a stern father giving last-minute advice to his children, Moses is trying to give the restless hoard standing before him some idea about how to conduct itself as a society.

Moses' Three Sermons
We're going to skim here. Of all the books of the Bible, *Deuteronomy* reminds me the most of when I was a child in church, struggling to stay awake, nearly blind with boredom, and I have no desire to recreate that experience here.

Moses' First Discourse is a polished review of all that the people have undergone and learned since leaving Egypt.

The Second Discourse gives us the final draft of the Ten Commandments (the rough draft is in *Exodus* 20). Chapter 7 of this discourse also firmly establishes the right of the Israelites to displace and if necessary destroy any peoples standing between them and the Promised Land ("Devour, then, all these peoples…show them no pity…" 7:16). You can be sure that modern Palestinians have read these passages with great interest.

Chapter 12 begins a shrewd catalog of rules, a constitution in effect, under which Israeli society is to be formed. This was touched upon in *Leviticus*, but here it is presented in a much more orderly and comprehensive fashion. In Chapter 15, for example, the mechanism of the Jubilee (see p. 46) and remission of debts is tightened and speeded up to provide for the wiping out of debts every seven years instead of every forty-nine. It even includes a primitive welfare system:

> *"Of course there will never cease to be poor in the land; I command you therefore: Always be openhanded with your brother, and with anyone in your country who is in need and poor.*

15:11

This point is expanded:

> *"When reaping the harvest in your field, if you have overlooked a sheaf in that field, do not go back for it. Leave it for the stranger, the orphan and the widow…"*

24:19

The text also slyly notes that the seven-year rule does not apply to debts held by foreigners ("from a foreigner you may exact payment," 15:3), and suggests that if this loophole is exploited shrewdly the Israelites "will be creditors to many nations and debtors to none," (15:6). This is the beginning of the long and bitter history of Jewish ingenuity with money. The stereotypes associated with "The Merchant of Venice" and the banking empire of the Rothschilds begin here.

Chapter 16 gives us some practical insight into Yahweh's

insistence that only unleavened bread be eaten with Passover meals. It is "the bread of emergency," bread that can be made quickly and readily stored. You make it at night and the next morning you're on the road, fleeing Egypt. No time to wait for the dough to rise. Besides, have you ever tried to fit a loaf of Wonder Bread into a backpack?

Chapter 18 offers an empirical, though unsatisfying, test to separate true from false prophets: make them predict something, and then wait to see if it comes true (18:22). That's fine if the prophecy is about rainfall this spring or how many sheep will die this winter. The problem is that with some of these guys you have to wait until the End of Time to find out if they were on the money or not.

Chapter 19 introduces a section called The Law of Retaliation. Apparently blood vengeance ("eye for eye, tooth for tooth" *Exodus* 21: 24) was a real problem in those days. Even something as innocent as someone falling from your roof could result in knife-wielding relatives coming after you. Thus the advice in 22:8 to "give your roof a parapet." Today we would call that an insurance stipulation.

Trying to bring some order to the endless rounds of bloodletting and vengeance, Moses decrees that three cities be designated as sanctuaries (the cities are not named) for those who have accidentally killed others:

> *"If anyone has struck his fellow accidentally, not having any previous feud with him (for example, he goes with his fellow into the forest to cut wood; he swings the ax to fell a tree; the head slips off the handle and strikes his*

> *companion dead) that man may take refuge in
> one of these cities and save his life."*

19:4-6

He also softens some of the savagery implied by the "eye for eye" refrain by introducing strict rules under which vengeance may legally be pursued. Here is the most intriguing of them:

> *"In the land Yahweh is giving you as your
> possession, if a murdered man is discovered
> lying in open country and it is not known who
> killed him, your elders and scribes must go and
> measure the distance between the victim and
> the surrounding towns, and establish which
> town is nearest the victim. Then the elders of
> that town are to take a heifer that has not yet
> been put to work or used as a draught animal
> under the yoke. And the elders of that town
> must bring the heifer down to a watercourse
> that is never dry at a spot that has been neither
> plowed nor sown, and there by the watercourse
> they must break the heifer's neck... And the
> elders of the town nearest the murdered man
> shall then wash their hands in the watercourse,
> over the slaughtered heifer. They are to
> pronounce these words, 'Our hands did not
> shed this blood and our eyes saw nothing...'*

21:1-8

In other words, "We wash our hands of it," another instance of you heard it first in the Bible. Pontius Pilate will employ this metaphor to distance himself from the guilt of Jesus' crucifixion.

Fear and Loathing of Women

Deuteronomy is a groaning smorgasbord of misogynistic delights. To be fair, we must admit that most cultures are guilty of oppressing women. The Hindus do it. The Muslims do it. The Chinese do it. And the Christians do it. Misogyny is older than the Bible, so it would be unfair to point at the Bible as the source of it in our culture. Still, the compilers of the Old Testament are second to none in codifying the inferior role of Israelite women.

It shows even in passages that are meant to demonstrate enlightened and fair treatment of women. Consider this, from a section on how to treat women captured in war:

> *"...if you see a beautiful woman among the prisoners and find her desirable, you may make her your wife and bring her to your home.... Should she cease to please you, you will let her go where she wishes, not selling her for money...since you have had the use of her."*

21:10-14

What a guy, huh? He won't take a penny for her since, as he modestly acknowledges, he has already "had the use of her."

Or how about the sub-section called "A Young Wife's Reputation." It's in 22:13-21, and here's what is says: If a newly-married man sleeps with his wife and afterwards declares her not to have been a virgin, then her father and mother must take her home and conduct an investigation. If they find that she was a virgin when she married and can produce a cloth to prove it, she will be found innocent. (How do you do that? Could Old Testament gynecologists travel backwards in time?) The punishment for the defaming husband is a hundred shekel fine and flogging. The reward for the girl is that her lying husband must take her back. I bet she's thrilled about that.

On other hand, if the girl's parents cannot prove their daughter was a virgin she is stoned to death. To review: if the husband is lying, he is fined, and the girl must go back to him. If the girl is lying, she is stoned to death. Sounds fair to me.

The Horror of Disobedience
Moses brings his second discourse to an end by rolling up his sleeves and giving the congregation a two-fisted, Bible-thumping (if he had a Bible) dose of the terrors they will be in for if they break Yahweh's laws. In a scorching roar that would have done Jonathan Edwards proud, he paints a vivid picture of the hell on earth that awaits disobedient Israelites.

> *"You will be accursed in the town and accursed in the country. Accursed will be your pannier and your bread bin. Accursed will be the fruit of your body, the produce of your soil, the increase of your cattle, the young of your flock. Accursed will you be coming in, and accursed going out."*

28:16-19

The rhetorical fire builds and builds.

> *"Yahweh will strike you down with consumption, fever, inflammation... The heavens above you will be brass, the earth beneath you iron."*

28:23-24

Finally, after two pages of this stuff, the text transcends mere rant and enters a realm of truly horrific imagery; it becomes a prose poem of damnation. In this passage Moses is prophesying that a great nation will rise up and lay siege to all of Israel's towns, literally starving the people into submission. Read this, if you dare:

> *"The most tender and fastidious woman among you, so tender, so fastidious that she has never ventured to set the sole of her foot to the ground, will glower at the husband she cherishes, even at her son and her daughter, and hide from them the afterbirth of her womb and the child she bears to eat them, so utter will be the destitution during the siege and in the distress to which your enemies will reduce you in all your towns.*

28:56-57

No modern horror story packs more despair into so few images.

The Third Discourse

Moses' presentation is almost done. Even as he speaks the people are quietly preparing for war. The Third Discourse makes it clear that the Ten Commandments are the text of a covenant that God is entering into with His people. Keep the Commandments and:

> *...you will live and increase, and Yahweh your God will bless you in the land which you are entering to make your own.*

30:16-17

But if you don't hold to the terms of the covenant, "...you will most certainly perish." (30:18)

But hey, this should be a *happy* moment. The Chosen People are camped at the edge of the Promised Land, preparing with quiet confidence for a conquest Yahweh assures them is certain. Moses, who knows that he's not going to accompany them into the Promised Land, is about to anoint a new leader, Joshua, who will lead the army over the Jordan River to victory. Yes, this should be a triumphant and happy moment.

But it's not. Yahweh tells Moses, and Moses relays the message to the people, that He has exercised His omniscience to peer into the future and He already knows that the Israelites are soon going to desert their faith, backsliding into libidinous pagan practices,

> *...playing the harlot, following the alien gods of the land they are invading. They will desert me and break this covenant of mine that I have made with them. On that day my anger shall blaze against them; I will forsake them and hide my face from them.*
> 31:16

Does it ever occur to God that people drift away from Him because He's just plain unpleasant and scary?

Exit Stage Left
Remember when I said earlier that Moses will take a long time to get off the stage? Well, the moment is at hand. He's even going to sing a song as his closing act. "The Song of Moses" foretells the destruction of the Chosen People and then their final restoration to blessedness after they have learned their lesson.

Anyway, he gets through it and adds a blessing to the tribes as well. Then Yahweh (figuratively) puts His arm over Moses' shoulder and leads him up Mount Nebo to die. From the mountaintop they can see across the Jordan River to Canaan. "This," says Yahweh,

> *...is the land I swore to give to Abraham, Isaac and Jacob, saying: I will give it to your descendents. I have let you see it with your own eyes, but you shall not cross into it.*

34:4-5

And with that Moses expires. Below, on the plains, the grieving Israelites are weeping and tearing their clothes. After a thirty-day period of mourning, Joshua, more general than prophet, reaches for his sword and shield and rises to his feet. With a rustling of weaponry the other men stand with him. It's time.

The Book of Joshua

Though we've graduated from the five mighty books of Torah, *The Book of Joshua* continues the story of the journey to the Promised Land. In fact, *Joshua* reads like the sports section, complete with a conquest score sheet and a real estate wrap-up.

The narrative structure is a bit like a World War II victory movie. The director focuses painstakingly on the signature battle, and then after we've seen for ourselves how devastating the victory is, the story speeds up, giving us only outtakes from the remaining battles, leaving the overall impression of a series of crushing victories.

The scene for the signature battle in *Joshua* is Jericho, famous today mainly for its harmonically sensitive walls. After a pair of spies report back to Joshua that the Canaanites are trembling in fear before the advance of the Israelite forces, Joshua gives the order to move out. As a sign that this is the selfsame Israelite mob that broke out of Egypt forty years before, they perform the trick that made them famous: the parting of the waters. In this case, when the priests carrying the ark of the covenant set their feet in the Jordan River the river stops flowing, piling up in a great watery mass to the north, "…and all Israel continued to cross dry-shod till the whole nation had finished its crossing of the river." (3:17)

Under Yahweh's direction, the army of the Israelites spends a week softening up the walled city, marching in circles around it, with the priests sounding their ram's horn trumpets. On the last day they march around it seven times. When the final circuit is complete the army comes to a halt and turns to face the walls. On Joshua's signal the soldiers all take a deep breath and let fly with their best war cry which, in conjunction with the trumpets' spittle-filled din, creates a killer sound wave. As the old spiritual says, "an' de walls dey came a tumblin' down."

With its wall demolished Jericho is defenseless. The residents are immediately placed under the ban. All the "men and women, young and old, even the oxen and sheep and donkeys" (6:21), are massacred.

Now the narrative begins ticking off the victories more and more rapidly. As the news spreads of the Israelite invasion, the various Canaanite kingdoms try different strategies to delay the inevitable. Some form alliances, others make offers of peace, mostly to no avail. The clever envoys of one kingdom, the Gibeonites, succeed in convincing the Israelites that they were beneath conquest and conclude a treaty before the Israelite leadership realizes that Gibeon was in fact one of the most important cities in the southern region. Grudgingly, acknowledging that they had failed to perform due diligence before signing the treaty, the Israelites agree to honor it, though they huffily inform the Gibeonites that forevermore they would never rise above the station of "serfs, woodcutters and water-carriers." (9:23-24)

---

[7] Getting into the subject of the Philistines is not really within the scope of this book. On the other hand, references to them are scattered throughout the Old and New Testaments, so something needs to be said about them. They were the bane of the Jews for centuries. From ca. 1200 BCE on they were the dominant cultural and military force in Canaan. They owned almost the whole western coast fronting on the Mediterranean Sea. They had a monopoly on iron weapons and tools. They forbade the Israelites from having their own smiths (13:19-22). If the Israelites wanted their tools sharpened, they had to come out of the hills and visit the Philistines. Today the very word Philistine is synonymous with boorish behavior.

And suddenly, it's over. The smoke clears. The Israelite warriors lower their swords and lances. The bottom line of the lengthy box score provided in Chapter 12 reads: Total Number of Kings Conquered, 31. There are a few holdouts, including the Philistines[7] on the coast, but Yahweh promises He will take care of them Himself.

Real Estate Wrap-Up
Time to divvy up the Promised Land among the twelve tribes. You'll recall that the Reubenites, the Gaddites, and the eastern half of the tribe of Manasseh had already elected to remain in the rich pasturage east of the Jordan. As agreed, they sent soldiers to help with the conquest of Canaan, so Yahweh is happy to keep His side of the deal. That leaves nine tribes among which to divide the land. It's done like an awards ceremony, with Joshua making complimentary little remarks about each tribe as its leaders approach him to accept their share. Only the House of Joseph sees fit to complain, saying its portion is too small. In response, Joshua throws another mountain into their portion, and slyly suggests that if they want more territory they can always go drive away the Philistines on the coastal plains with their "iron chariots and superior strength." (17:18) Suddenly the sons of Joseph are finished talking. No one is about to volunteer to take on the Philistines.

The great horde of Israel is ready to disband, each tribe to retire to the portion assigned to it. Never again will the Israelites live, travel, or fight as one. In fact never again will the twelve tribes even think of themselves a single people. Yet there is one last thing to be done.

The Great Assembly at Shechem
Yahweh and Joshua feel the need, before the Israelites break camp

for the last time, to renew the covenants that have bound this people together since the time of Abraham. They call for one last community assembly at Shechem, which will be the first capital. Ultimately this assembly will be a futile gesture, because the fatal flaw of the Israelites (and by extension all humanity) is that they always choose the expedient over the eternal. Solving the immediate problem—be it an opposing army, a pestilential disease, or a crop failure—will always be more important to them than oaths to this off-putting and bristling deity that insists on calling Himself the only God in the universe. *Of course* the Israelites know better than this. They can see with their own eyes that there are gods all over the place in Egypt and Palestine. It's a *marketplace* of gods! And unlike Yahweh, these gods are specialists. There are gods of weather, gods of fertility, gods of war, and so on. You can go to them with a specific problem, and with the right prayers and sacrifices, expect to get results.

At least that's what the people believed. From this point until the time of King David the central conflict among this Chosen People will be whether or not they will continue to follow the commandments of a God that promises them eternal dominion over…what? History? Mankind? Yahweh never spells it out. The temptation to give in to the seductive blandishments of the pagan gods and secular leaders who promise to solve their immediate problems will be at times too strong to resist.

The Great Assembly at Shechem was an attempt to head off this conflict. Already the tribes east of the Jordan (the old men, women, and children left behind while their warriors conquered Canaan) have succumbed to worshipping the local gods, and it is only with great difficulty that they are pressured into (temporarily) renouncing them.

Now at the Great Assembly the tribes all gather for the last time. Joshua, a mini-Moses, recounts the history of their association with Yahweh, the special privilege of being elected the Chosen People. Like Moses bringing forth the stone tablets of the Ten Commandments, Joshua produces a new covenant engraved in stone, and sets it under an oak tree (24:26). He demands that then and there, for the final time, the people choose whether or not to serve Yahweh. Of course they all proclaim their undying love for Him, and the Great Assembly is pronounced a success. "Then Joshua sent the people away, and each returned to his own inheritance." (24:28)

Judging by what happens in the next few books, most of the people there at Shechem shouting their loyalty to Yahweh must have had one hand behind their backs, fingers crossed.

The Book of Judges

> *"In those days there was no king in Israel, and every man did as he pleased."*
> Judges 21:25

Now it's time for the most rootin' tootin' book in the Bible, save perhaps for the fiery bestiary that is *Revelations*, which we will explore in due course. We're in about 1380 BCE now, the very earliest days of the Israelite state. *Judges* presents the trials and tribulations of this period, when Yahweh attempted to manage the day-to-day affairs of this— probably the best word is "federation"—by means of a series of priest-leaders called "judges." When you see the word "judge" think "war lord."

The core problem, from an administrative point-of-view, is how closely should Yahweh be involved in the day-to-day affairs of His people. He has already shown Himself to be a poor steward of quotidian affairs. His eye tends to stay on the big picture. For Him, history is on fast-forward and He can't wait to get to the end. You don't want to be bothering Him about your infertile ewes. Yet, as we begin *Judges*, Yahweh hasn't conceded that point yet. For the moment He wants to run the whole show, using the judges as His puppet representatives.

The lesson of *Judges* is to show how poorly things go under this system. By the time the period of the judges has run its course (between 350-450 years) the people will be so sick of it they'll be begging the last judge, Samuel, to give them a king.

Judges is presented as a series of capsule narratives summarizing the events of each judge's reign. Some of them are quite long, some unbelievably brutal and bloody, some dreadfully boring, some quite short. The entire reign of the judge Shamgar, for example, is rendered in a single sentence:

> *He routed six hundred of the Philistines with an*
> *ox goad; he too was a deliverer of Israel.*

3:31

Dude was good with an ox goad.

Most of the stories are linked by variations on a single numbing refrain: "The Israelites did what displeases Yahweh." That's the signal for the nearest pagan king to enslave them, for Yahweh to withdraw His protection, and for the next judge to burst upon the scene to save the day.

Several of these dozen stories read like they were written on the spot, and the details can be appalling, or comical, or both. For example, Yahweh calls upon a judge named Ehud to rescue the Israelites from the oppression of a Moabite king named Eglon. Ehud, a left-hander, makes a special dagger for himself, about a cubit long (twenty-one inches), and straps it under his robe. He arranges to present a tribute to Eglon, who is described as a "very fat man." After presenting the tribute, Ehud asks for private word with the king. The writer clearly savors what happens next:

> *Then Ehud, using his left hand, drew the*
> *dagger he was carrying on his right thigh and*
> *thrust it into the king's belly. The hilt too went*
> *in after the blade, and the fat closed over the*
> *blade, for Ehud left the dagger in his belly;*
> *then he went out through the window.*

3:21-23

Before any of the king's people can get through the locked doors, Ehud is long gone. Soon he returns with an army that crushes a demoralized Moabite force of ten thousand "tough and seasoned fighters." Yay.

Under the reign of Jephthah, there was a war between the tribes of Ephraim and Gilead, who spoke Hebrew using different dialects. Gilead won the war, and set up check points to "cut Ephraim off from the fords of the Jordan." (12:5) Whenever a man approached a check point, the soldiers demanded that he speak the word "Shibboleth." (The original meaning of shibboleth is irrelevant, but if you must know, it is the part of a plant that contains the grain.) Since the Ephraimite dialect did not include an "sh" phoneme, Ephraimites pronounced Shibboleth as "Sibboleth." Anybody who pronounced it that way was slaughtered on the spot. "There perished in this way 42,000 men of Ephraim." (12:6) I tot I saw a puddy tat.

By far the most famous story in *Judges* is that of the Israelite superman Samson, told in Chapter 16. Obviously a much-embellished folktale, Samson vanquishes every Philistine attempt to kill him until the harlot Delilah learns the secret of his strength: his long hair. She cuts it, he is captured, and his eyes are put out. Held in captivity, he regains his strength as his hair grows back. The Philistines, meanwhile, have made him into a freak show attraction, a blind strongman performing feats of strength. One day an audience of about 3,000 crowds into and onto a building to watch the show. At some point Samson is placed between the two main pillars supporting the building. He pushes them over, killing himself and everyone in attendance. The end.

And so it goes in *Judges*, one gratuitously brutal story after another.

So the judge system did not work, and soon it will change. But first there is the four-page *Book of Ruth*.

The Book of Ruth

The Book of Ruth begins the drum roll that will reach its crashing climax with the emergence of David, the greatest king in Israel's history. No one knows when it was written, but the setting is during the time of the Judges, sometime after 1380 BCE. It's a feel-good story about a newly-widowed girl who migrates from the land of Moab to Judah in search of a husband.

Imagine how powerless she is! First of all, she's a woman, and it can't get much worse than that. Secondly, she's a widow, so although she's quite young she's still no virginal flower, and thus not very marketable as a bride. Thirdly, she's a foreigner.

Starving, she ventures into the corn fields during harvest time, seeking to find food for herself and her mother-in-law Naomi. You'll recall that the law allowed the poor to follow behind the harvesters, gleaning the few grains that fall to the ground. Even so, as a completely defenseless woman, Ruth knows she's in danger of being raped.[8]

Boaz, the kindly owner of the corn fields, spots the girl and asks who she is. When told, his heart is touched. He approaches her and tells her to stay in his fields, where he has ordered his servants not to "molest" her. At lunchtime, he invites her to eat by his side, offering her bread and wine. You can see where this is going.

A few days later, at Naomi's advice, she sneaks under Boaz's bed covers and curls up at his feet. That pretty much finishes Boaz off.

---

[8] This heart-rending predicament is what Keats was referring to in his *Ode to a Nightingale*: "Ruth amid the alien corn."

When he awakes and finds this stunning girl at his feet, he knows he must have her. But Boaz is determined to follow the rules. Legally, he's not first in line for her. A distant relative of Ruth's family has the first right of refusal. There's a certain amount of legal mumbling before the relative agrees that Boaz can "redeem" Ruth.

"So Boaz took Ruth and she became his wife." (4:13) Presently she has a son whom Boaz names Obed. And guess what? Obed will be the father of David's father Jesse. The drums of history beat a little faster.

The First & Second Books of Samuel

I Samuel and *II Samuel* are a single story, and that's how I'm going to treat them. It's the best story in the Bible, a true tragedy bristling with adventure, great characters and great writing. Most scholars place the writing (or assembling) of it around 600 B.C.E., about the time Homer was clearing his throat to recite *The Iliad* and *The Odyssey*. It ranks right up there on the list of great world literature.

Samuel is the grumbling old priest who is the last of Israel's judges. His job is to mediate between Yahweh and the Israelites to ensure that Yahweh gets worshipped properly and the people get their needs met, an arrangement that has never been very stable and is about to fall apart entirely.

This is still very early in Israelite history, about 1050 B.C.E. Israel is not yet a nation in the full sense of the word. Since taking possession of Canaan in about 1400 BCE, they've been living as a loosely-knit federation of tribes. The only persons they recognize as having anything like sovereign power are the priest-judges.

But the people are getting restless with the priest-judge system. These "leaders" had become a venal and self-serving class of men—woozy with wine and fat from eating free food. Listen to how the priest sons of Eli—one of the last priest-judges—comport themselves around the altar:

> *Now the sons of Eli were scoundrels; they cared nothing for Yahweh nor for the rights of the priests as regards the people. Whenever a man offered a sacrifice, the priest's servant*

> *would come with a three-pronged fork in his hand while the meat was being cooked; he would thrust this into the caldron or pan, or dish or pot, and the priest claimed for his own whatever the fork brought up.*

2:12-14

How long do expect people to put up with that kind of stuff?

We're looking at an organizational failure. Yahweh is the CEO, and the priest-judges are vice-presidents. They report only to Yahweh. The problem is, Yahweh doesn't care about the problems of daily living. He's busy running the universe and determining history. And since Yahweh doesn't care about the day-to-day life of the people, neither do the priest-judges. They're only concern is to keep the offerings coming.

Again and again the people quietly return to worshipping the smaller gods with more narrow job descriptions. Baal's good at weather, for example; and Astarte is good at fertility.

Something needs to change.

Long Live the King
As Samuel is getting old, his days as a judge coming to an end, he appoints his sons Joel and Abijah to be the next judges. That's the final straw. The sons are widely hated ("…they wanted money, taking bribes and perverting justice" [8:3]) and the people refuse to accept them. In fact, they demand another kind of governance entirely. "'So give us a king to rule over us, like the other nations.'" (8:3 and 8:5-6)

In a matter of a verse or two it's all taken care of. The Israelites agree to put aside their Baals and Astartes, Yahweh quickly vanquishes the encroaching Philistines, and just as quickly agrees to provide them with a king.

With that, a terrific hump in Israelite history is gotten over. The experiment with a God-managed society is over. The people may be pleased, but Yahweh displays some hurt feelings ("…they have rejected Me" [8:8]) and Samuel is disgusted. "Consider then what a very wicked thing you have done in the sight of Yahweh by asking to have a king," he says in 12:18.

In any case the thing is done. From an organizational point-of-view, a new position—king—has been created, answerable to both Yahweh and the people. The job description of the priest-judges is reduced to merely "priest."

And so it is that Saul, a terrifically complex and conflicted character, makes his way into the story. The son of a wealthy herder, it is in the course of chasing down a lost donkey that he runs into Samuel, who has been waiting for him. Samuel empties a phial of oil on Saul's head, kisses him, and tells him Yahweh has big plans for him.

Samuel calls together all the leaders of all the tribes and tells them it's time to select a king. They throw lots, and after a few rounds Saul (surprise!) comes up as the winner. Everyone shouts "Long live the king!" and goes home. At first you get the impression that nothing's changed. Saul returns to the fields and herds of his father. He's been given no specific duties. And not everyone is thrilled at the choice of this untested young man as their king. Saul wonders if he has any real authority or not. He's about to find out.

One day as he is coming in from the fields behind a team of oxen, a messenger arrives to report that the mountain village of Jabesh-

Gilead is under siege by the Ammonites.

> *And the spirit of Yahweh seized on Saul when he heard these words, and his fury was stirred to fierce flame.*
> 11:6-7

On the spot he orders a national mobilization. He chops his team of oxen into little pieces and sends the pieces across the land with the threat to do the same to the oxen of any man who refuses to serve. Yeah, baby! Suddenly the young man is acting like a KING! In no time an army of 330,000 falls in for inspection. With Saul leading them, they smash the Ammonites (11:11), and Saul in effect takes actual, as well at titular, possession of the crown.

Can't Catch a Break

Despite this success, almost immediately Saul's reign begins to go sour. It is as if—and the narrative takes no great pains to conceal this—Samuel and Yahweh conspire to trip him up, even though they were the ones to pick him in the first place.

Saul's basic offense seems to have been a tendency to take spiritual matters into his own hands. In one of the first recorded instances of church-state conflict, Saul, a king, and Samuel, a priest, fall out over the issue of who can make burnt offerings to Yahweh.

It happens just before a great battle with the Philistines. Samuel was supposed to meet Saul to make a burnt offering to Yahweh. Saul waits a whole week, and when Samuel still didn't show Saul made the offering himself. Samuel, of course, arrives as exactly this moment, and denounces Saul for usurping his role. At this point (13:7-15) Samuel withdraws his support from Saul. Yahweh, however, is apparently still with him because Saul goes on to win a great victory against the Philistines. But Yahweh's favor is about to be withdrawn.

'When I say all of them, I mean *all* of them'

The Amalekites, whose army Saul has just defeated, have a special place on Yahweh's list of who's naughty and nice. They were among the peoples who had contested the Israelites' passage across the desert in Exodus. But the Amalekites tried not to just block the Israelites, but to exterminate them. (*Exodus* 17) Yahweh hasn't forgotten that, and he now orders Saul to exterminate *them*. It's called being "put under the ban" and as we've seen before, it means that every living thing is to be killed, "man and woman, babe and suckling, ox and sheep, camel and donkey." (15:3)

But when the time comes, Saul can't quite bring himself to do it, at least not entirely. He spares the Amalekite king and keeps the best of the Amalekite livestock. Then he goes off to Carmel, "to raise himself a monument." Raise *himself* a monument? Isn't that a little presumptuous? Doesn't he know that he's already in big trouble for not killing the king and keeping the livestock?

Too late now. As quickly as that Yahweh is done with Saul. "I regret," he says, "having made Saul king, for he has turned away from me and has not carried out my orders." (15:11)

When Samuel finally catches up with him, Saul pleads his case. He only saved the Amalekite king and the animals as an offering to Yahweh. (15:20-21) "Is the pleasure of Yahweh…in sacrifices or in obedience?" asks Samuel. You can safely bet that's a rhetorical question. Saul goes on: I was going to put them under the ban, but I was afraid of my people (presumably the booty issue came up; soldiers like to pillage). Samuel is not moved. "Yahweh…has rejected you as king of Israel," he pronounces. (15:26)

And Samuel's not finished:

> *Today Yahweh has torn the kingdom of Israel*
> *from you and given it to a neighbor of yours*
> *who is better than you.*

15:28

A *neighbor?* Who could he possibly be talking about? (Hint: He's good with a sling.)

Meanwhile, Saul is a dead man walking. You would expect that he would be given five minutes to clean out his desk before being escorted out of the building by security. But it's not like that. His reign goes on for years and years. In fact, the narrative concedes that as far as accomplishments go, Saul was a pretty successful king. One sympathetic passage inventories his accomplishments:

> *Saul consolidated his rule over Israel and*
> *fought against all his enemies everywhere:*
> *against Moab, the Ammonites, Edom, Beth-*
> *rehob, the king of Zobah, the Philistines;*
> *wherever he turned he was victorious. He did*
> *great deeds of valor; he defeated the*
> *Amalekites and delivered Israel from the power*
> *of their plunderers.*

14:47-48

The Once and Future King

No matter. Yahweh and Samuel are moving on. Yahweh sends Samuel to Bethlehem (yes, *that* Bethlehem) to anoint a son of Jesse as the next king of Israel.

There's a brief bit of charming melodrama about how David is identified. Everyone in Bethlehem is excited, because the word is out that one of Jesse's sons is going to be named the next king. Eventually Jesse comes into town with his sons in tow, to present them to Samuel, who, after looking them over, rejects them all. "Are these all the sons you have?" Samuel asks. (16:11)

Jesse and his sons look at each other. Well, Jesse says, there is one more. But he's too young, too small. We didn't even bring him.

"Send for him," says Samuel. When the boy arrives, of course he's the one. Samuel anoints him on the spot. A shining new chapter of Jewish history—in fact, the most shining of all—is about to begin.

David, aware that the favor of Yahweh has been conferred upon him, confronts his first problem: what is he supposed to do? Though in Yahweh's eyes he is the king of Israel, everybody else thinks Saul is. David has to be careful. By one account (16:14-23,) he hires on as a musician to help soothe Saul's fits of madness (Yahweh has sent an "evil spirit" to bedevil Saul). The other account (17:12-22) has David traveling to Saul's camp with supplies from Bethlehem for his brothers on the battle line.

In any event, he is on the scene when Goliath of Gath, all ten and a half feet of him, issues his challenge. This, of course, is one of the most famous stories in the Bible. It seems obvious that it was an old and favorite story even when it was written down by the author(s) of *1 Samuel*, for it is told with a kind of childlike reverence for each delicious detail. We learn, for example, the exact weight of each piece of Goliath's armor and weaponry. His bronze breastplate weighed about a hundred pounds. "The shaft of his spear was like a weaver's beam, and the head of his spear weighed six hundred shekels of iron [about twelve pounds.]" (17:7)

The narrative tries to work up some anxiety about David's safety. Saul insists that David wear the king's own armor. But the boy finds the stuff so heavy and cumbersome that he cannot even walk. In the end, he goes out to face Goliath with no more than his famous sling and the five smooth stones. He and Goliath exchange ritual threats and insults (Goliath: "...I will give your flesh to the birds..."; David: "...I will cut off your head..."). The sling whizzes around and David lets fly with a stone. It penetrates Goliath's forehead (17:49), and the giant falls over, stone-dead. Like that, David is a great hero.

Saul, who does not yet realize that David is the one Yahweh has selected to replace him, rewards him by making him one of his commanders. David immediately establishes himself as a military superstar, and a new hit song sweeps the land, the refrain of which makes Saul's teeth grind:

> *Saul has killed his thousands, and David his tens of thousands.*

18:7

From here on in, Saul and David are adversaries. David is like a young buck circling a harem guarded by an aging elk. He knows that he doesn't have to fight, but just stay out of trouble and wait. Saul knows this too.

Saul's dilemma is classic tragedy. He overreached himself by making a burnt offering before the big battle with the Amakelites, then ignored the order to lay them under the ban. Finally, he displayed a bit of hubris by raising a monument to celebrate the victory. Now he is paying the price, and he knows it. He even knows that it's not David's fault that Yahweh has selected him. But he hates David anyway, and hates himself for hating him. He's been abandoned by his God, and he is filled with self-loathing because he knows it's his fault. His suffering is acute, and there's no relief in sight. But he's still the king, and he's still trying to do his job.

Meanwhile David's exploits are grabbing the headlines. When Saul's daughter Michal confesses her infatuation with him, Saul gives his blessing to the marriage, with the malicious proviso that David must first present the king with the foreskins of a hundred Philistines (18:25). *That* should keep him out of the household for a while. But in no time David is back, having in his youthful excess gathered proof that not one hundred, but two hundred Philistine soldiers won't be riding their horses for a while. Saul grudgingly accepts him as his son-in-law.

At this point Saul succumbs to the mental illness that will be his special hell until his death. His own good conscience tells him that David is a nice young man who means him no harm, is loved by the people and is under Yahweh's special protection. But the "evil spirit" Yahweh has sent to madden Saul goads him into doing things that he hates himself for. One moment he'll be listening to David strumming the harp and singing a psalm and the next moment he'll seize a spear and try to impale him with it (19:9-10).

David knows it's time to flee. There's one fascinating detail in the story of his escape. Michal, Saul's daughter and David's wife, learns that Saul has sent men to kill him. She lets David down through a back window, and he takes off. She then grabs a little household statue (called a "teraphim,"), puts some goat hair on it, and throws a blanket over it. When Saul's men arrive she tells them that David is ill in bed, and shows them the strange hairy shape under the blanket (19:11-17). The soldiers fall for this bit of trickery and go away. But look what has just happened here. That teraphim is a *god! In the camp of the King of the Israelites, people are hoarding little pagan gods in their tents.* Perhaps they have no more significance than good luck charms, but it's amazing how stubborn this practice was. And Yahweh doesn't even seem to care. Go figure.

Superboy

From now on David is the unequivocal star of the narrative. Everything he does has that aura of dash and athleticism that you would expect a military culture-hero to have.

He takes refuge in the mountains with his band of loyal men. They have little difficulty in avoiding Saul's clumsy search-and-destroy missions, though an incident from one of these missions is worth re-telling: Saul halts his forces in front of the very cave where David and his men are hiding. Saul goes into the cave to relieve himself (to "cover his feet," in the Biblical euphemism,) and as he is doing so David creeps forward and cuts the border off Saul's cloak. When Saul leaves the cave to rejoin his forces, David runs out after him and stands at the cave entrance holding up the bit of cloth he has cut off. He calls out to Saul:

> *"Why, your own eyes have seen today how*
> *Yahweh put you in my power in the cave and*
> *how I refused to kill you, but spared you....you*
> *must acknowledge frankly that there is neither*
> *malice nor treason in my mind."*

24:11-12

That is matinee melodrama. Zorro couldn't have played it better.

Desperate for some kind of guidance, now that Yahweh is no longer even acknowledging his prayers, Saul decides to consult a necromancer known as the witch of En-dor. She causes the recently-deceased Samuel to rise up from the earth wrapped in a cloak. Saul tells him his troubles—the Philistines are pressing hard, Yahweh has abandoned him. Samuel, annoyed at being disturbed, lets Saul have it with both barrels:

> *"And why do you consult me, when*
> *Yahweh...has snatched the sovereignty from*
> *your hand and given it to your neighbor,*
> *David... Yahweh will deliver Israel and you,*
> *too, into the power of the Philistines.*
> *Tomorrow you and your sons will be with me...*

28:16-19

The next day's battle on Mount Gilboa goes just as Samuel foretold. Saul's forces are cut to pieces. Three of his sons, including Jonathan, David's closest friend, are killed. Presently the Philistine fighters close in on Saul himself. He is wounded by an arrow. Seeing that the end is near, he turns to his armor-bearer and says "Draw your sword and run me through with it. I do not want these uncircumcised men to come and gloat over me." The armor-bearer is too rattled to comply, so "Saul took his own sword and fell on it" (31:4), a stunt that is much easier to describe than it is to do. Try falling on, say, a broom-handle. Do you just lean on it? Would that be enough force? Are you supposed to jump on it? How do you prop it up?

In any case, when the Philistines find Saul's body, they cut off the head (it will go on tour in their country,) and nail the body to a wall. Remember Jabesh-gilead, the mountain village that Saul saved in his first action as king? When these people hear what had been done with Saul's body, they march through the night to reclaim it and give him an honorable burial. (31:11-13)

So it ends for Saul and the *First Book of Samuel*. I was fascinated that it would finish on this dogged note that, despite everything, there were those who believed Saul was a worthy king and a good man. He just never seemed to grasp the complexities of how to worship and obey Yahweh, who seems as embarrassed as angered by Saul's mistakes.

Meanwhile, the Philistines think they have Israel on the run. Yeah, but look who's king now!

The Second Book of Samuel

David's reign as king is the high point of Israelite history. The biblical narrative will never again see a ruler or prophet so beloved by Yahweh as David…except for Jesus, of course; but we'll deal with him later.

II Samuel begins with the Israelite community yet again in a great state of turmoil and flux. David has just won a great victory against the Amalekites, but Saul has just died at the hands of the Philistines. The people of Judah, the largest and most powerful of the Israelite tribes, have no trouble accepting David as their king. But the tribes still loyal to Saul's line withdraw to their northern territories.

Right in here things get a little confusing. Basically, the tribes divide into two warring countries—"Israel" to the north and Judah to the south. The idea of the Israelites as a single people is gone.

> *So the war dragged on between the House of Saul and the House of David, but David grew steadily stronger, and the House of Saul ever weaker.*
> 3:1

David originally sets up his court at Hebron, but after seven years he moves it to Jerusalem, which is pretty much in the center of Judah, one of the original Israelite regions. The Kingdom of Judah—soon to be known as the land of the Jews— is beginning to take shape. One big problem remains, however. Yahweh's personal penthouse, the Ark of the Covenant, is still in storage. And getting it to Jerusalem turns out to be a tricky and dangerous exercise.

The Ark is being temporarily stored at a town called Baalah. David, accompanied by an honor guard of thirty thousand men, goes there to reclaim it. Setting the Ark on a brand-new cart, they set out for Jerusalem in a joyous parade:

> *David* [and all his men] *danced before Yahweh with all their might, singing to the accompaniment of lyres, harps, tambourines, castanets, and cymbals.*
> 6:5-6

Sounds like they're having a great time. A smidgen of fear is probably in the mix too, as well there should be. Look what happens next: a poor innocent named Uzzah is walking next to the Ark as it rolls along. They come to a little dip in the road, and the Ark begins to tilt. Uzzah instinctively puts out his hand to steady it, "and for this crime God struck him down on the spot." (6:7) Say what? The kid was just trying to *help!* It's as if Yahweh is reminding His people what a strict, angry, and arbitrary deity He is.

David gets it. He "went in fear of Yahweh that day." (6:9) Suddenly he changes his mind about taking the Ark all the way to Jerusalem. Instead, he decides to cart it to the nearby house of a friend, Obed-edom of Gath. Clearly, David wants to see how dangerous it is to be around the Ark on a daily basis, and Obed is the test case. Some friend David is, huh?

Three months later Obed and his family still haven't been fried, so David decides it's safe to bring the Ark to Jerusalem. More dancing, more joyous noise, more cymbals and tambourines. But this time David plans to be very, very careful. After *six steps* he stops the whole parade and sacrifices an ox and a fat sheep. How's that for first-class appeasement? But there's more! Not only does David offer the sacrifices, but he strips down to his loin cloth and begins to dance, "whirling around Yahweh with all his might." (6:14)

So hysterical is David in his livid, fearful frenzy that he is an embarrassment to his own wife, Michal who goes out to meet him, saying:

> *"What a fine reputation the king of Israel has won himself today," she said, "displaying himself under the eyes of his servant maids, as any buffoon might display himself."*

6:20-21

David, undeterred, replies "I shall dance before Yahweh and

demean myself even more." (6:22) And he does. Meanwhile, as punishment for her disrespect to David, Yahweh makes Michal a barren woman. He never did like her much, anyway, because she was a closet pagan. Remember that teraphim she produced to hide David when Saul was after him?

Think of the sheer terror and hysterical ecstasy Yahweh stirs up in the hearts of His people. It's not a pretty picture. Abusive husbands use this same technique of unpredictable outbursts of love and anger to make slaves of their wives. When you're not sure if you're going to get a caress or a slap, it makes you crazy.

Anyway, the Ark of the Covenant is finally installed in Jerusalem, so it's all good. What's next?

Housekeeping
Yahweh wants to settle down:

> *I have never stayed in a house from the day I*
> *brought the Israelites out of Egypt until today,*
> *but have always led a wanderer's life in a tent.*

7:6-7

There's a plaintive tone in there that almost makes you feel sorry for Him. Here Yahweh has been taking care of the universe all this time, and nobody's even built a house for Him? It's time to set things right. David and Yahweh make a deal. If David will build a house on earth for Yahweh to abide in, Yahweh promises to make the line of David Israel's kings.

> *And when your days are ended and you are laid*
> *to rest with your ancestors, I will preserve the*
> *offspring of your body after you and make his*
> *sovereignty secure.*

7:12-13

This contract is referenced in *The Psalms,* which according to tradition were all written (and sung) by Daved: "I have founded your dynasty to last forever…" (*Psalms* 89:29)

Bathsheba
Most of the rest of *II Samuel* goes by in a blizzard of wars, adultery, assassinations, political maneuvering, intrigues, and betrayals. And guess what? A lot of this is *fun*. Just listen to the first line of Chapter 11:

At the turn of the year, the time when kings go campaigning…

"When kings go campaigning"? It's like a sport. War season. You nurse your grudges all winter, then launch a cathartic war in the spring. It's what kings do!

It's funny that the text should say this right at this moment, because the war in question—a campaign against the Ammonites—is one that David did not personally engage in. What was he doing instead? He's watching Bathsheba, the wife of one of his soldiers, taking a bath. (11:2-3) And that's only the beginning. This is an astonishing story, showing a king abusing the powers of his office in the worst way.

Here's what happens: Having watched her bathe, David, tumescent with voyeuristic lust, sends for Bathsheba, sleeps with her and gets her pregnant. There's no sign that he feels guilty about this, but he does know that he could get into trouble. So he tries to appease Bathsheba's husband, Uriah, by calling him back from the battle line and encouraging him to take it easy for a while: "Go down to your house and enjoy yourself." (11:8) Maybe he's thinking that if Uriah sleeps with his wife he won't figure out that David is the father of the baby. But Uriah doesn't feel good about partying at home while his comrades are fighting and dying in battle. Instead, he sleeps on the ground by the palace door. When David remonstrates with him the next morning, Uriah replies:

> *"Are not the ark and the men of Israel and Judah lodged in tents...in the open fields? Am I to go to my house, then, and eat and drink and sleep with my wife?... I will do no such thing."*

11:11-12

Clearly, bribing Uriah isn't going to work. So David reverses his strategy. He sends Uriah back to the front lines with a letter instructing the general, Joab, to put Uriah in the thick of the fight and "then fall back behind him so that he may be struck down and die." (11:14-15) And that's exactly what happens.

Can a king's behavior be any more despicable? Compared with this crime, this murder, Saul breaking the rules by preparing a burnt offering is nothing! For that sin, Saul lost his crown and ultimately his life. What happens to David? Nothing more than a severe scolding. In the end he says he's sorry and Yahweh forgives him. His only punishment is the death of the child he had by Bathsheba. Later she bears David another child, whose name will be Solomon.

So what is the lesson here? *Obedience!* Yahweh will forgive almost anything but disobedience. As well-intentioned and pure of heart Saul was when he made that burnt offering in *I Samuel* 13, it was an act of disobedience. On the other hand, David, for all his cheating and intrigues, never fails to do what Yahweh commands. For this, he is remembered as the greatest king in Jewish history.

Absalom

Now that David's comfortably settled as the king, he begins to have sons (he will have nineteen in all) and boys being boys, they start to get in trouble. The story of Absalom, the third son, covers seven chapters and is a slurry of several narrative threads. One is the story of a family tragedy. Another is the story of family treachery. Yet another is the smoldering hatred of David by the northern tribes[9] still loyal to Saul's line.

Anyway, two of David's sons, Amnon and Absalom, are in conflict. Amnon has developed an obsession with his sister Tamar, whom he rapes. (13:14) For this, Absalom arranges Amnon's murder, then flees the country to escape his father's wrath. (13:23-34) After several years, David relents and Absalom is permitted to return to Jerusalem. The text is ambiguous on the next point, but apparently David never fully forgives Absalom, or Absalom feels insulted by David's remoteness.

In any event, Absalom starts to stir up trouble. He sets up a little stand outside the gates of the city and solicits the business of people who have come to Jerusalem to consult with the king. (15:1-6) In this way, he begins to develop a little base of power for himself. Eventually, he travels to Hebron, names himself king, gathers an army and marches on Jerusalem.

---

[9] This is one of those 'you-can't-tell-the-players-without-a-scorecard' moments. Let's sort it out the best we can. The northern tribes (ten in all) have coalesced into a loose federation called Israel. The remaining tribes, Judah and Benjamin, have formed a nation in the south called Judah. At this point, both Israel and Judah regard David as their king. But the people of Israel are discontent under David's rule, and soon that will come to a head.

Apparently Absalom's forces are formidable, for David flees the city. As Absalom takes possession of Jerusalem he produces Saul's grandson Meribaal[10], and thus cements the support of the northern tribes. (16:1-4) After a brief respite and some minor intrigues among courtiers and spies, Absalom gathers his army and goes in pursuit of David. (17:24-25)

By then David has re-organized his forces and prepares to meet Absalom. The battle is joined in the Forest of Ephraim, where David wins a great victory. (18:1-8)

He gives orders for Absalom to be left unharmed, but it's tough to hold back fighting men when their blood is up. It's an odd little story: Absalom flees the field of battle on a mule. He gallops under an oak tree and accidentally catches his head in the branches. He is still hanging there, alive, when some men led by David's general, Joab, come upon him. As Absalom dangles, the men argue about what to do with him. One, remembering David's order, wants to spare him. But Joab can't hold himself back and sticks three lances into Absalom's heart. (18:9-17)

That ends the war, but does not heal the federation, which is in a shambles. The remnants of Absalom's army still don't want David for their king, though they don't dare attempt to raise another of their own. Muttering dangerously, they withdraw to the north. The schism between Judah and Israel is more clearly defined than ever.

As David consolidates his power he goes one step too far. He orders a census of the still-defiant northern tribes. A census means

---

[10] Notice that "baal" at the end of his name. It's *so hard* to shake the pagan gods!

several things to the people being counted, none of them good. First, it is a show of raw power—'I can send my officials to count your people and you can't stop me.' Also—just as bad—it can be the basis for taxation. Thirdly, it is a way of assessing just how much of a threat the people being counted are. In the case of the northern tribes, David's officials report that "Israel numbered eight hundred thousand armed men capable of drawing the sword." (24:9) That's undoubtedly a huge exaggeration, but the point is that Israel, though defeated, is still plenty dangerous.

Even Yahweh agrees that this humiliation of the northern tribes is too much, and decides to chastise David. He gives David his choice of three punishments: three years of famine, three months of being pursued by his enemy (presumably Israel), or three days of pestilence. David chooses pestilence, and the result is a plague that kills seventy thousand men (it kills lots of women and children too, but as always, we don't count them).

On that unnerving note, *II Samuel* comes to an end. It's time for David to retire, and that's where the next book starts.

The First & Second Books of the Kings

Let's review. *I & II Samuel* is primarily the story of how David rose to the monarchy of Judah which, according to the priest-editors of the Old Testament, was the high point of Jewish history. This brief glorious moment was in 1000 BCE, give or take a few decades.

I & II Kings is about how all that comes undone.

The Struggle for Succession
As the story opens David is in his dotage, shivering in bed. You can tell that he's still popular because—get this—they assign a beautiful young girl to lie on him to keep him warm. Today, we call that health care coverage.

(1:2-4) Palace intrigues are seething all around him. Two of David's sons (by different wives) are vying to succeed him. Adonijah takes the early lead by surrounding himself with the power elite—among them the great general Joab—and basically anointing himself king. But Bathsheba (remember her, toweling off on the roof?), the mother of Solomon, rushes to the king's bedside to complain about Adonijah's behavior, and David, who never could say "no" to Bathsheba, names Solomon his successor. (1:40)

Solomon is the last king to rule over Israel as a single nation. His ambition is to make Jerusalem the shining jewel of the Middle East. He envisions an array of public works projects, chief among them the construction of a suitably majestic temple to house Yahweh. Using the military resources that David had built up, and the census that David had taken of the northern territories, he institutes a policy of forced labor to carry out his projects. Eventually, this will prove to be a mistake.

Like many American presidents, Solomon does best on the international scene. He shows himself to be a clever statesman, allying himself with Egypt by marrying one of the pharaoh's daughters. He also negotiates a treaty with neighboring Tyre (Lebanon) which gives him access to both a vast lumber supply (the legendary cedars of Lebanon) and Lebanon's technically superior workforce. Eventually, he will have seven hundred wives, most of them foreign, each one of them representing a sort of living treaty. As backup, he also kept a stable of three hundred concubines.

If there was ever proof that Biblical head counts were habitually inflated, this is it. Seven hundred wives and three hundred concubines? Here's a Bible rule-of-thumb for headcounts: knock off the zeros.

Solomon the Wise
Solomon's wisdom was legendary, and this story is a prime example: Two prostitutes who live together give birth at practically the same time. Soon after, one of them in her sleep rolls over her baby and kills him. Quietly, she swaps her dead baby for the live one. In the morning the two women argue fiercely over whose baby died. They go before Solomon to adjudicate the matter. He listens to them argue for a while, then calls for a sword. "'Cut the living child in two,' the king said,' and give half to one and half to the other.'" (3:24-26) Quickly, one of the women steps forward and pleads for the king to give the child to the other woman. Solomon immediately declares her the true mother, because only a mother would rather lose her child than have it put to death.

Solomon the Builder

Job number one on Solomon's agenda is to build the Temple. Half of Chapter 5 and all of Chapter 6 are devoted to the project. It takes seven years, and multitudes of workers. One portion of his indentured workforce he sends to Tyre to gather lumber and learn the art of construction. Another part he sends to the mountains to quarry stone. The tour of duty was one month in Tyre, two months at home, in relays of ten thousand workers per cycle.

The foundation of the building was probably quarried and dressed stone. Lebanese cedar beams supported the roof. Ornamental carvings of gourds and rosettes and pomegranates were everywhere. The whole was covered in gold gilt. The interior was filled with bronze furniture. Sounds like it was pretty impressive.

But don't go home yet, indentured workers! After the Temple project is completed, the project of building a palace begins, taking thirteen years to complete.

Solomon the Pagan

Of course, those seven hundred foreign wives brought their own gods with them. In an implausible turn of events, Solomon starts worshipping those gods as well.

> *Solomon became a follower of Astarte, the goddess of the Sidonians, and of Milcom, the Ammonite abomination.... [He] built a high place for Chemosh, the god of Moab...*

11:5-7

At this point Yahweh turns his back on Solomon, though He relents enough to allow Solomon to finish out his reign.

Reality Check

Let's indulge ourselves and read between the lines for just a second. You'll recall that at the end of *Numbers* the leaders of a very confident Israeli army divided Canaan (soon to be Israel) among the twelve Israelite tribes. The tension between the northern tribes and the southern tribes (mainly Judah) had been out in the open ever since Saul (from the northern tribe of Benjamin) was anointed the first king of Israel. There were several issues simmering here. First, Judah was by far the largest and most powerful of the tribes, and the Judeans weren't happy about having to bow to a northern king.

Secondly, Jerusalem was in Judah. Everyone acknowledged that the Temple in Jerusalem was the most important place to make offerings to Yahweh. But the priests of Judah went farther than that. They maintained that only offerings made at their Temple were valid. This meant that the priests of the northern tribes had to travel a long way to make offerings; it also in effect made them inferior to the priests already ensconced in Jerusalem.

Another issue was the program of forced labor initiated by Solomon, the king of Judah. Most of this labor force came not from Judah but from the northern tribes. Originally implemented for the Temple project, this practice of forced labor lasted for the entire forty years of Solomon's reign and created much resentment.

The Final Straw
Solomon dies peacefully, and his son Rehoboam inherits the throne. He gets one last chance to re-unite the country. The northern tribes assemble at Shechem, the ancient northern city where Abraham himself once made sacrifices to Yahweh. The intent of this gathering is to decide who the northern tribes will recognize as king: Rehoboam, Solomon's son, or Jeroboam, the favorite of the northern tribes. Who would you put your money

on?

Addressing the assembled host at Shechem, Rehoboam puts his foot in his mouth, big time. When asked what he intends to do about his father's much-hated forced labor policy, he replies:

> *"So then, my father made you bear a heavy burden. I will make it heavier still. My father beat you with whips; I am going to beat you with loaded scourges."*

12:11

That didn't go over well. The assembled host replies as one, saying:

> *"What share have we in David?*
> *We have no inheritance in the son of Jesse.*
> *To your tents, Israel!*
> *Henceforth look after your own house, David!"*
> 12:16

Soon after Jeroboam is acclaimed king of Israel. For the northern tribes, that was it.

A word about regional and ethnic names: Until now, Israel has been the name of the Israelite nation. David was King of Israel, Solomon was King of Israel. But with the elevation of Rehoboam to king, the question of what and to whom the name Israel applies begins to morph. Within a relatively short amount of time, the name Israel applies only to the lands held by the northern tribes. That makes Rehoboam the king only of Judah, or "Yehudah" in Hebrew. The people of Judah called themselves Yehudim, which translates into English as Judeans, which we have further abbreviated to Jews.

Almost immediately Judah and Israel descend into a state of war, at first a cold war, but then it quickly heats up. The northern king, Jeroboam, realizing that it was important to eliminate the obligation to journey to Jerusalem to make offerings, sets up his own altars. In no time the people of Israel revert to paganism, with all the usual offensive practices: worshipping golden calves, employing male prostitutes (12:28-30 & 14:24), and—worst of all—treating Yahweh as if He were just another god. Remember, this is history as written by Judean priests/editors. It would be a whole different story if we could hear the other side—but that story has disappeared.

The narrative line—which up to here has hovered in uneasy equilibrium between the claims to righteousness of both sides—here begins to tilt. The whole experiment of the Chosen People starts to slide toward extinction. As Chapter 15 opens, somebody presses the fast-forward button, and kings of Judah and Israel begin to fly by at an alarming rate. It's like sorting through a collection of baseball cards. The names change, the statistics change, but the structure remains the same. Here's the formula: 'In the ____ year ____ became king. He reigned for ____ years. In every way he copied the example of (the previous king) by doing what is displeasing to Yahweh. Then he slept with his ancestors and his son ____ succeeded him.' There are thirty-nine cards in this collection, and hardly any are worth mentioning.

Elijah and Elisha
As Chapter 17 opens, the March of the Unworthy Kings is put on hold for a while in order to tell the stories of two of the Bible's great prophets, Elijah and Elisha. Basically, this is a collection of miraculous folk tales designed to dramatize Yahweh's dominion

over the scruffy little pagan deities that the Jews and Israelites can't seem to leave alone.

Ahab is the unfortunate Israelite king (874-853 B.C.E) under whose reign Elijah makes his reputation. Suddenly, without preamble, Elijah pops up, declaring that, because of Ahab's faithlessness, drought and famine are about to descend upon the land. Quickly he flees to the desert to escape Ahab's wrath. Out in the wasteland he stays on the move, led by Yahweh to tiny watering places and provided with food by magical ravens—bread in the morning, meat in the afternoon.

Presently, Ahab and his people are reeling under the punishments of drought and famine. They are just at the point where they are looking sideways at their horses and mules. Elijah chooses this moment to return. He challenges Ahab's pagan priests to a rain-making contest on Mount Carmel. This a great scene, depicted with obvious relish: Elijah alone against 400 priests of Baal, with "all Israel" for an audience.

The rules of the contest are simple. Both sides are given a bull to prepare for sacrifice. The god who signifies his pleasure by incinerating the offering will be acclaimed the true god. Mockingly, Elijah stands aside and lets the priests of Baal have first try. All morning and into the late afternoon they shout and perform their rituals:

> *"O Baal, answer us!" they cried, but there was no voice, no answer, as they performed their hobbling dance around the altar they had made.... Elijah mocked them. "Call louder," he said, "for he is a god: he is preoccupied or he is busy, or he has gone on a journey;*

> *perhaps he is asleep and will wake up."*
> 18:26-28

> That lifted sneering lip of the word "hobbling" is nice.

But despite their imploring, no rain arrives in response to the Baal priests' efforts. Finally they give up and it's Elijah's turn. After a certain amount of throat-clearing, Yahweh sets Elijah's bull ablaze. The people immediately proclaim Yahweh as the true God, and Elijah promptly slaughters the incompetent pagan priests, all four hundred of them. (18:40) Everybody quiets down and waits for the rain to start.

There seems to have been an anxious moment or two. Elijah has a man go up to the top of the hill to look toward the sea for signs of a storm. On the seventh such trip the man reports a cloud "small as a man's hand, rising from the sea." (18:44) With that, Elijah knows he's pulled it off. Elated, he tells Ahab he'd better hurry and get on his chariot before the rain makes the road impassable.

> *Ahab mounted his chariot and made for*
> *Jezreel. The hand of Yahweh was on Elijah*
> *and, tucking up his cloak, he ran in front of*
> *Ahab as far as the outskirts of Jezreel.*
> 18:45-46

I love that last bit: Elijah, ecstatic and relieved, pulling his cloak up and outracing the chariot.

Soon after, Yahweh informs Elijah that he has located his successor, a young man with (unfortunately for us) the almost identical name of Elisha. Elijah finds him plowing his father's fields and immediately claims him as his apprentice. The poor kid doesn't even get to go home and say good-bye to his parents.

The Second Book of Kings

The bumpy narrative ride continues. Meaningless miracles, feckless kings—the detritus of Jewish history is being dumped at our feet. We'll just have to sort through it.

Elijah is preparing to meet his Maker. He is restless and irritable; he wants to be alone, and he begins to wander about the land, as if looking for the right place to die. But Elisha, along with an entourage of fifty prophets, refuses to leave his side. The old prophet leads the entourage to the Jordan River, where he and Elisha stand on the bank together. Behind them, at a distance, the other prophets fearfully huddle. Everyone knows that something big is about to happen.

Elijah rolls up his cloak and smacks the water with it. The river parts and he and Elisha cross over, leaving their brethren behind. Elisha, sensing that there's not much time left, puts in his request: "Let me inherit a double share of your spirit." (2:10) Even as they speak the swing-low-sweet-chariots-of-fire come tumbling down from the firmament and with a cry Elijah is swept away as Elisha shrieks "My father! My father!" (2:12) Elijah's clothes lie on the ground, and Elisha tears them in his grief. Just like that, he is the Main Prophet.

Now Elijah, despite his reputation, produced a relatively small number of miracles in his career. But they were good ones, each with a specific purpose and with a little lesson attached (the lifting of the drought, for example, re-kindled King Ahab's faith in

Yahweh). With Elisha it's a different story. He had asked for a double dose of Elijah's powers, and he got it. He starts performing miracles immediately. He seems to think that his *job* is to produce miracles, whether they mean anything or not. No prophet before or since matches Elisha for pure miracle productivity.

Here's one of his first ones: on his way back from the events at the Jordan River he is accosted by a group of small boys who keeping shouting: "'Go up, baldhead!' they shouted. 'Go up, baldhead!'" Here's how Elisha deals with the problem. "Two she-bears came out of the woods and savaged forty-two of the boys." (2:23-25) *Now* who's bald, huh?

Elisha's contribution to *II Kings* is a marathon magic show. Here are some of the highlights: First he repeats a few of his mentor's miracles, as if to establish his *bona fides:* he parts the Jordan River (2:14), helps a widow who is running low on olive oil (4:3), and brings a young boy back from the dead. (4:18-37) Then he moves on to original material. Passing through Gilgal, he de-toxifies a pot of poisoned soup (4:38-41) and multiplies some loaves. (4:42-44) Later, he cures the commander of the Aramean army of leprosy, and when one of his servants secretly accepts payment for the cure, passes the disease on to him—though he lets him keep the money. (5:1-27)

One of my favorites is the Miracle of the Axe-Head. In this one Elisha comes to inspect some new quarters the prophets are building for themselves on the banks of the Jordan. As he is watching, an axe-head slips off its handle and falls into the river. "Alas, my lord," laments the prophet, "it was a borrowed one too." (I love that. Losing a borrowed axe-head is even worse than losing your own. You lose the axe-head and the respect of the person who loaned it to you.) Almost casually Elisha points a stick at the spot where the axe-head sank and up it pops like a bar of Ivory soap. (6:1-7) Later he lifts a siege of Samaria[11] by generating the sound of a great army thundering to the rescue, creating panic amid the enemy's troops, who run screaming into the desert. (6:24-33 & 7:1-8)

From the standpoint of carrying on with the business of advancing the story the most important act Elisha performs is not a miracle but merely a priestly function. He summons one of the junior prophets and tells him to go to Ramoth-Gilead and anoint an army commander named Jehu as the new king of Israel.

Jehu's first job is to "wipe out every male belonging to the family of Ahab." (9:1-9) Ahab must have been an exceptionally blasphemous king. Yahweh seems to want to go to extra lengths to destroy him and everyone around him.

Painted Jezebel
Even Jezebel, Ahab's queen, doesn't escape Yahweh's wrath. She was guilty of egging Ahab on as he conducted his atrocities. Today, she is remembered as "painted Jezebel," the iconic wickedly beautiful and arrogant temptress. Here is what happens: Jezebel, knowing that Jehu is coming after her,

> ...*made up her eyes with kohl* [powdered antimony, which yields a black and glittering concoction used to darken the eyelids] *and adorned her head and appeared at the window* [in the manner of a prostitute]. *As Jehu came through the gateway she said, "Is all well,*

---

[11] The starvation was so severe that people were paying eighty shekels for a donkey head! Wow. I can remember when donkey heads were only ten shekels.

> *Zimri[12], you murderer of your master?" Jehu looked up to the window and said... "Throw her down." They threw her down, and her blood spattered the walls and the horses, and Jehu rode over her.*

9:30-33

For a devout Christian, there isn't a worse insult than to call a woman a painted Jezebel.

The Beginning of the End
Jehu's reign began around 840 BCE. Dramatically, we're almost to the low point in the history of the Chosen People, though chronologically the kingdom of Israel persists for another century, while Judah lingers on for two and half centuries.

Judah's fall might have occurred at about the same time as Israel's but for the fiery imprecations of a prophet named Isaiah, who inspired the Judeans to beat back an Assyrian assault in about 700 BCE. I mention him now only because a large and important book of the Old Testament is written in his name.

Other moments of note in *II Kings* include the discovery of the original scroll containing *Book of Deuteronomy* under the reign of Josiah in 622 BCE (Chapter 22). This occurred during the course of some repairs to the Temple, and triggered a brief return of devotion to Yahweh.

Chapter 23:10 makes the first reference to the infamous Valley of Ben-Hinnom, which is thought to be the inspiration for the concept

---

[12] Zimri currently held the record for the shortest reign in the Bible—eight days. Jezebel is taunting Jehu with the comparison.

of Hell. We'll investigate it in more detail later.

So it is done. The smoke lies low over the empty land. The children of Abraham are in the hands of their enemies. The first Diaspora is underway. The Assyrians conquer Israel in 721 BCE and scatter its people to parts unknown. The Mormons are said to believe that Native Americans are descended from some of these tribes. Some Islamic scholars believe the lost tribes settled in the area of what today comprises northeast India, Kashmir, and Afghanistan.

Judah is conquered by the Babylonians in 587 BCE and the Judeans were deported, for the most part, to Babylon, though some end up in Egypt. (The Babylonians didn't bother with the old, infirm, or mentally deficient, who were allowed to remain in Judah.)

The rest of the Old Testament comes from the writings of these Judean exiles in Babylon.

The First and Second Books of the Chronicles

Together, *1 Chronicles* and *2 Chronicles* cover the history of the Jews from the reign of David to the fall of Jerusalem at the hands of the Babylonians. It's *exactly* the same material covered by *II Samuel* and *I & II Kings*, except that the editor of *Chronicles* acknowledges at the end that Cyrus, King of Persia, released the Jews (in 538 B.C.E) to return to Jerusalem to rebuild the Temple.

The main difference between these two versions of the same history? In *Kings* the stories are well told. In *Chronicles* the stories are stripped of all the blood and drama and strong characters and replaced by the droning voice of a pedantic priestly writer. So let's move on to *Ezra* and *Nehemiah*, shall we?

The Book of Ezra and Nehemiah

In 538 BCE Cyrus the Great conquered Babylon, renamed it Persia, and issued an edict freeing the Jews to return to Judah and rebuild their Temple (the edict even included generous reparations of gold and silver). Ezra and Nehemiah were the two principle leaders of the repatriation.

Ezra
Ezra, a priest, sees his job as the re-education of the exiles on what it means to be Jewish. He is shocked at how ignorant they are. They don't even understand Classical Hebrew! Probably the most important single event recorded in *Ezra and Nehemiah* is Ezra's public reading of the Torah (the Jewish name for the first five books of the Old Testament; in Christianity it is known as the Pentateuch), which he translates into Aramaic as he reads, so that the people can understand (*Nehemiah* 8). After Ezra, Jewish priests would be known as rabbis, men with a deep understanding of the Torah, whose job it was to keep the Jewish community aware of the sacred laws and sacred history.

Even worse than their ignorance of the Torah is the fact that many of the returning exiles bring their Persian wives and children with them. It makes Ezra want to tear his hair—literally. Here's how he puts it:

> *At this news* [of the foreign wives] *I tore hair from my head and beard and sat down, quite overcome. All who trembled at the words of the God of Israel gathered around me, when faced by this treachery of the exiles.*

9:3

Of course the men are forced to give up these pagan wives and their families.

Nehemiah
Nehemiah is an administrator whose principle job is to oversee the Temple restoration project. He also works with Ezra to reinstate the various social and religious rules that set a strictly Jewish community apart from others.

Regional jealousies arise over the project of restoring the Temple. The Samaritans to the north (occupying the land formally owned by the Israelites) first want in on the project (there's a lot of money flying around; the project is lavishly funded by the Persians). When the Samaritans are rebuffed, they do a one-eighty and start complaining that the restoration is a danger to the region, that the Jews are a war-like and defiant people etc. etc. This regional bickering is patiently adjudicated over a number of years by three Persian kings. In the end the Judeans win, and get even more funding from the Persians.

Much of the material in *Ezra and Nehemiah* is lists: lists of the returning exiles, lists of those who helped on the Temple project, lists of those who couldn't confirm their Judean ancestry, lists of those who had brought foreign wives. The lists are compiled with an eye to the future, to establish provable lineages. It's a little like the lists of names you see on plaques on the walls of privately-funded projects.

By the time *The Book of Ezra and Nehemiah* ends, the Temple is restored (though not to its former glory) and Jerusalem is once again populated by Jews busily learning how to be Jewish.

That is the end of the Old Testament as history. But there is much more to come. Primarily the remaining books were written by or about prophets, among them the towering figure of Isaiah. Also we have some rip-roaring folk tales to relate, as well as a couple of books that are not that far from just being cartoons.

Esther

The book of *Esther* is the tale of brave girl risking all to prevent the genocide of her people.

Queen Vashti of Babylon has just insulted King Xerxes I by refusing to display herself to a bunch of drunken men at the king's banquet. He banishes her from the court and instructs his officials to gather the most beautiful virgins in the land to compete for who will be the next queen. Mordecai the Jew, a high official at the court, recommends his adopted daughter Esther. She easily wins the competition and is acclaimed the new queen.

Mordecai's rival in palace politics is Haman, the royal vizier and second only to the king himself in power. Mordecai, knowing his daughter is queen, refuses to prostrate himself before Haman. Haman decides his wounded pride can be assuaged not just by the murder of Mordecai, but the annihilation of all the Jews, "root and branch." (3:13) Haman goes before the king, railing about this stubborn and disrespectful people who, unlike all the other conquered peoples, refuse to be assimilated into Babylonian society. They consistently ignore the king's laws, and persist in following their own strange practices. Xerxes, who doesn't seem that interested, tells Haman to "do what you like with them." (3:11) The vizier begins to lay plans for the genocide. He casts lots (a little like throwing dice or flipping a coin; the Hebrew word for lots is purim) to determine the day of the Jews' destruction. He orders a special gallows built just to hang Mordecai. You can almost see him rubbing his hands.

When Mordecai learns of Haman's intentions, he begs Esther to go before the king and plead for the lives of her people. When she replies that it is death to approach the king without being summoned, he tells her "Do not suppose that, because you are in the king's palace, you are going to be the one Jew to escape." (4:14) In other words, you'll die either way, so why not try to save yourself *and* your people?

After three days of fasting, she approaches the king's chambers and enters, unannounced and unsummoned.

> *Raising his face, afire with majesty, he looked on her, blazing with anger. The queen sank down. She grew faint and the color drained from her face, and she leaned her head against the maid who accompanied her. But God changed the king's heart, inducing a milder spirit. He sprang from the throne in alarm and took her in his arms until she recovered, comforting her with soothing words.*

5:1-1

It's all over. He'll do anything she asks.

Eventually, after some pointless dithering the writer throws in to build suspense (she insists on preparing two banquets before she'll say anything), Esther reveals to the king the dire plot to have the Jews wiped out. Her argument, though couched in terms of abject humility, is cleverly framed: a) if all the Jews are to be killed, then he will have to kill her too; b) the king is about to lose a significant portion of his population, and all the taxes and productivity that goes with it, without receiving any compensation; and c) if you love me you'll do this for me. (7:3-5)

Haman, who is seated at the banquet table with them, must feel the delicacies he has just consumed churning in his stomach.

Xerxes demands the name of the man who is planning this outrage. "Why, this wretch Haman!" she says, pointing to him." (7:6)

Shortly after that Haman is hung upon the very gallows he had erected for Mordecai, and Mordecai inherits Haman's position of Chancellor. That's a wrap. Everybody's got what he or she deserved. The end.

But there is a problem. The order to exterminate the Jews has already gone out. It may be too late to countermand it. The kingdom is too vast, the army units too scattered. The only hope is to alert the Jewish community. Quickly, Xerxes issues a decree that gives the Jews the right to assemble in self-defense if threatened. (What? They didn't have that already?) Sure enough, when the attacks come the Jews are ready and the annihilation goes the other way. Seventy-five thousand anti-Semites are remanded into the care of their pagan gods over the next two days.

Today, the feast of Purim is celebrated on the fourteenth day of the Hebrew month of Adar.

The Book of Job

This is one of the Wisdom books, meaning that it is focused on teaching and has little or no historical content. There's no telling when *Job* was written. Best guess is somewhere around 600 BCE, which could possibly place it during the time of the first Diaspora (between ca. 580 and 530)—a fitting moment in Jewish history for a story about a man trying to endure a series of what seem like unjustified attacks on him by God.

The basic structure is like a Socratic dialogue (though Socrates hadn't been born yet): four men in an earnest debate in search of philosophical (or in this case religious) truth. Their discussion revolves around questions like: What right does a man have to question God? Does a man have a right to expect his God to act fairly?

A Difficult Man
Contrary to commonly received notions about Job, he is emphatically *not* the model of the long-suffering good man, tirelessly worshipful, unshakable in his faith. And the contest is not between God and Satan for possession for Job's soul, as we've been taught, but between Job and God for the authority to say what's fair. From the outset Job is intransigent, unrepentant, and outraged that he of all people should have these senseless sufferings inflicted upon him. While his "friends," like a Greek chorus, implore and exhort him to give in and admit his basic sinfulness, Job repeatedly demands to know why he has been singled out for persecution. He goes even farther. Job insists that *God Himself* ought to be held accountable for His actions! It is this stark drama of a man calling on his God to submit to the law He Himself has laid down that is the heart of the story. It's like a

child demanding that his parents live by their own rules. It sounds right, but as all parents know, it's impossible.... I don't know why, it just is. Now stop arguing with me. Go upstairs.

The first two chapters are fun to read because they have a folktale charm to them. Thus we have Job, pure-as-the-driven-snow. He is blessed with seven sons and three daughters, is quite wealthy, and pious to a fault. Looking down on Job are God and Satan:

> *So Yahweh asked him, "Did you notice my servant Job? There is no one like him on the earth: a sound and honest man who fears God and shuns evil."*
> *"Yes," Satan said, "but Job is not God-fearing for nothing, is he?...But stretch Your hand and lay a finger on his possessions: I warrant you, he will curse You to Your face."*
> 1:8-12

They sound like two young English gentlemen preparing to lay a wager. And lay it they do. The next day Satan showers calamity after calamity upon the hapless human. By nighttime Job is poor and childless. But his faith isn't weakened. (1:21)

Satan and God resume their conversation. Okay, says Satan, that didn't do the trick. But if you let me torment his body, the human will surely forsake You.

So God gives Satan permission to go after Job's health. By the end of the next day the poor man is sitting in an ash pit using a piece of pottery to scrape at the ulcers Satan has covered his body with. Even his wife mocks him. Still, he refuses to curse God, saying that you have to take the bad with the good. (2:10) Up to this point, Job seems pretty much to be the perfect, humble, pious guy they told us about in Bible class.

The Dialogue

This where the philosophical disputations begin. Three friends, Eliphaz, Bildad, and Zophar, have heard of Job's plight and arrive to offer their sympathy and consolation. Solemn with sadness and pity, they sit by him for a whole week without saying a word. They listen as Job utters his lament ("May the day perish when I was born," [3:3]). One interesting thing the lament reveals is that the Jewish notion of an afterlife still has not progressed past the concept of Sheol, that giant morgue to which all souls are consigned, whether sinful or virtuous. When Job says he wishes to die, Sheol is where he thinks he would end up.

At this point his faith begins to crumble a little bit. He wonders why he was brought into this world in the first place.

> *Why make this gift of light to a man who does not see his way, whom God balks on every side?*
> 3:23

Finally his friends speak up. They scramble to reprimand him. They are shocked at his heretical groans. Eliphaz says, in effect, that since the basis of the ethical system handed down to us by God is that good men are not punished, by definition Job *must* have committed a sin. In fact, it's impossible *not* to commit sins if you are a man. So God is not punishing you, He is *correcting* you. "Happy the man whom God corrects!" (5:17)

Job's reply? If this is love, I'd rather die. "May it please God to…do away with me." (6:9) Then, in what may be the most dramatic utterance of the whole book, he wonders what's the point?

> *What is man that you should make so much of him,*
> *subjecting him to Your scrutiny,*
> *that morning after morning You should examine him*
> *and at every instant test him?*
> *Will You never take your eyes off me*
> *long enough for me to swallow my spittle?*

7:17-19

Bildad, the next friend, mechanically repeats Eliphaz's argument that Job must have done something wrong, because God "neither spurns a stainless man, nor lends His aid to the evil." (8:20) This so infuriates Job that he escalates the level of his blasphemy. Screw it, he says. It doesn't matter whether he's sinned or not because, "this I dare to say: innocent and guilty, He destroys all alike." (9:22)

In Chapters 12, 13, and 14 Job escalates his rebellion. His argument goes like this: Okay, let's grant for a moment that I have sinned. But since God made me, does He not bear responsibility for this? Yeah, who's guilty now? (12:9-10)

If you were hoping that we are about to get into the question of free will, forget it. It just gets raised this one time, and is never pursued.

I'll See You in Court
Then Job then challenges God to submit to the justice system.

> *I will proceed by due form of law,*
> *persuaded as I am that I am guiltless.*
> 13:18

> *Then arraign me, and I will reply;*
> *or rather, I will speak and You shall answer me.*
> *How many faults and crimes have I committed?*
> *What law have I transgressed, or in what have I offended?*
> 13:22-23

"I will speak and you shall answer me." The dude is *suing* God! Is that chutzpah or what?

A Taste of Heaven (and Hell)

Just as Chapter 14 is coming to an end, a fascinating new concept makes its first appearance in the Bible: resurrection. At this juncture, Job is reduced to asking for a time-out. Here's what he says:

> *If only you would hide me in Sheol,*
> *and shelter me there until your anger is past,*
> *fixing a certain day for calling me to mind,*
> *for once a man is dead can he come back to life?—*
> *day after day of my service I would wait*
> *for my relief to come.*
> 14:13-14

It's fascinating to watch such powerful concepts as Resurrection, Heaven and Hell evolve as we work our way through the Bible. They all seem to be rooted in Sheol, early Judaism's primitive idea of where the dead go. Here we see the first hint of what eventually will become the doctrine of resurrection: "…for once a man is dead can he come back to life?"

In the meantime, the cycle of disputation between Job and his three friends goes on and on for another thirteen chapters, the oratory unrelieved by new ideas or new rhetoric.

The New Kid on the Block
In Chapter 31 Job is insisting—for the millionth time—on his innocence. He cites his virtuous acts and asks again and again 'What have I done?'

Just as we think we're about to go out of our minds with boredom, a new character pops up: Elihu, a younger man who explains that he has kept silent all this time out of respect for the elders, but can hold his peace no longer. His is a formidable new voice, jolting the depleted dialogue back to life. Here is a synopsis of Elihu's argument as it is put forth in Chapters 34 through 37: *You, Job, are a man, and therefore express yourself in words. But God is the Creator, and is free to express Himself in any way He pleases. He may come to you in dreams, for example, or in visions. You've been sitting here for days demanding He express Himself in words—the manner to which you are limited. If you open your eyes and ears you may find He has been answering you all along.*

It's actually a new argument! It sets Job on his heels.

Finally, with a casuistic flourish, Elihu finishes Job off with a mean little paradox. Even if Job had not committed a sin before, he says, the very act of questioning God is sin enough.

> *For to sin he adds rebellion,*
> *calling justice into question in our midst*

> *and heaping abuse on God.*
34:37

That's so unfair! A parent hits a kid. The kid wails "What did I do?" The parent says "You asked that question."

You Know Not Whereof You Speak
Yahweh decides it's time to end this flea circus. He's let these little specks argue about the meaning of the universe long enough. You get the feeling that from His point-of-view it's almost cute, hearing these little voices become shrill as they debate how God should behave. But enough is enough. Time to put everyone in his place.

Reciting from His résumé, Yahweh reminds Job how much He has to know to run the universe. His responsibilities run the gamut from the vast:

> *Have you ever in your life given orders to the morning*
> *Or sent the dawn to its post*
> *Telling it to grasp the earth by its edges*
> *And shake the wicked out of it?...*
38:12-13

to the very specialized:

> *Do you know how mountain goats give birth?*
39:1

As always, it's an unfair argument. It's like saying to a child, 'Do you know how to drive a car? No? Then shut up.'

Elihu goes on like this for four chapters. It's the argument of an exasperated parent who doesn't feel respected and wants to restore the proper balance of authority. 'Do you know how hard I work to give you this nice house, these nice clothes? You don't seem to appreciate...' etc. etc. Every child in history has rolled his eyes at this argument.

It's even a little embarrassing that Yahweh stoops to this line of defense, because it *doesn't mean a thing!* If you're God, you're *supposed* to run the universe. It's your job. Making your child feel insignificant because he can't do your job is bullying.

And Job reacts like a defeated, bullied child. He practically wets himself trying to get back in Yahweh's good graces:

> *I am the man who obscured your designs*
> *With my empty-headed words.*
> *I have been holding forth on matters I cannot understand*
> *On marvels beyond me and my knowledge....*
> *I retract all I have said,*
> *And in dust and ashes I repent.*

42:3-6

Job, the man who tried to use his God-given gift of reason to understand God's inexplicable actions, has been put in his place.

The Book of Job ends on this embarrassing note. I guess the best that you can say for books like these in the Bible (the patently unfair treatment of Saul in *I Samuel* is the other example that comes to mind) is that at least they have the courage to raise certain difficult questions even if they have to duck back behind a curtain of impenetrable authority to avoid dealing with them.

The Psalms

Psalms is the Jewish hymnal, meant for public performance at the Temple in Jerusalem. It consists of 150 songs and poems. Some are quite old, going back as far as the beginning of the first millennium. Others seem to refer to much later times, as late as the post-exilic return to Jerusalem after 530 BCE. Still others have a kind of "I've seen everything" air that seems to take place in no time at all. The tradition is that they were all written and performed by King David, and at least some probably were.

Reading the whole book of *Psalms* can be a numbing experience. But these poems are not made to be read. They're meant to be sung or chanted, and not all at one time. So reading them at one pass is, in a sense, unfair. But there are a few things to point out.

Often in these poems we re-encounter the good old fashioned Yahweh, the bristling, dangerous, hungry Deity of the Pentateuch. Omnipotent, unpredictable, quick to anger, capricious and unaccountable—this is a Deity to keep you on your toes. A God like this needs a lot of assuaging. Here is a passage from Psalm 71, which is introduced as "An Old Man's Prayer":

> *You have done great things;*
> *who, God, is comparable to you?*
> *You have sent me misery and hardship,*
> *but you will give me life again,*
> *you will pull me up again from the depths of the earth,*
> *prolong my old age, and once more comfort me.*

> *I promise I will thank you on the lyre,*
> *my ever-faithful God,*
> *I will play the harp in your honor,*
> *Holy One of Israel.*
> 71:19-22

That sounds like a servant tactfully reminding his master about the pension plan he's been promised.

As a matter of fact, what I hear in *Psalms* overall are fragments of voices, each calling to a different aspect of his Deity. There's something pitiful and haunting in how long these people have been knocking on the Temple door, afraid it won't open, afraid that it will. The sum of all their prayers is, 'Please don't hit me. I love You unconditionally. I try to obey Your rules. Sometimes You don't appear to go by them Yourself. But I am weak and flawed and in no position to say. So just protect me, okay?'

But the spirit of defiance in the Jewish character is never far away. *Job* is its exemplar, the stubborn man exasperated by the ceaseless scrutiny of his cruel God. There is some of that here too. "Look," says the author of Psalm 39,

> *I am worn out with the blows you deal me.*
> *You punish man with the penalties of sin,*
> *like a moth you eat away all that gives him*
> *pleasure.*

39:5-11

Hell's Bells
The ideas of Hell and Resurrection take on a little more shape as they weave in and out of some of the psalms. The place of the dead is still Sheol, but it is also called the Pit; and it no longer is a

neutral resting place for good and bad alike, but a place to be avoided. Here are some hints of Hell:

> *For you will not abandon my soul to Sheol,*
> *nor allow the one you love to see the Pit...*
> 16:10

> *Do not be deaf to me,*
> *for if you are silent, I shall go*
> *down to the Pit like the rest.*
> 28:1

And Resurrection:

> *Yahweh, you have brought my soul up from Sheol,*
> *of all those who go down to the Pit you have revived me.*
> 30:3

> *But God will redeem my life*
> *from the grasp of Sheol, and will receive me.*
> 49:15

And even a little taste of Heaven:

> *And I will dwell in the*
> *House of the Lord forever.*
> 23:6

The Once and Future King
Then there's Psalm 22. It contains the line, "My God, my God, why have you deserted me?" (22:1) It just so happens that those are the very words that Jesus cries out when he is dying in agony

on the Cross. How can that be? Some conservative Christian commentators regard Psalm 22 as a prophecy of Jesus' crucifixion, and that by saying those words he is fulfilling the prophecy.

No doubt. But, as an educated Jew (see *Luke 2:47-48*, where as a boy he wows the wise men at the Temple), was he quoting from a Psalm that he was familiar with, and thus *consciously* fulfilling the prophecy? Or are these words the spontaneous expression of the despair he is feeling at that moment? Or both?

A little stage management seems like a definite possibility, either on Jesus' part (but it seems mean-spirited to think that), or on the part of whoever wrote or edited the Gospels, especially the earliest one, *Mark*. For some early Christians it was important to show that Jesus' career was foreshadowed in the Old Testament, and important as well to associate him with King David, from whose line the Messiah is supposed to descend. Having Jesus speak this line from a poem written by David accomplishes both these things.

The Book of Proverbs

Proverbs consists almost entirely of small bits of advice and observations addressed to upperclass Jewish men. It would have been the favorite book of Polonius, the slightly ditsy advisor in Shakespeare's "Hamlet," he of "Neither a borrower or a lender be." Many of *Proverbs* epigrams are addressed to younger men ambitious to establish themselves in the world. They include advice on how to behave in the company of rich and powerful persons, even going so far as to give tips on table manners:

> *When you sit to dine with a ruler,*
> *note well what is before you,*
> *and put a knife to your throat*
> *if you are given to gluttony.*
> *Do not crave his delicacies,*
> *for that food is deceptive.*
> 23:1-3

Careful! The rich man sets delicacies before you to see how much restraint you have. You don't want to look up from your fourth éclair to see him frowning. An image of the ideal Jewish man forms as you read these little nuggets of wisdom: he is rich, honest, hardworking, reluctant to criticize others but severe on his sons, and he never, *never* co-signs on loans.

Naturally one of the strongest themes is that good, God-fearing people are also successful in worldly matters; that success is one of God's rewards for spiritual uprightness. That's very convenient for the upper classes, isn't it? Acquiring wealth and power is almost the same as praying.

But this doesn't exactly accord with strict theology, and so *Proverbs* often vibrates like an old car, trying to contain its contradictions. For example, in 10:4 it says:

> *The slack hand brings poverty,*
> *but the diligent hand brings wealth.*

But 10:22 politely disagrees:

> *The blessing of Yahweh is what brings riches,*
> *to this hard toil has nothing to add.*

Or how about 15:23?

*When a man has a ready answer he has joy too;
how satisfying is the apt reply!*

Compare that to 17:27:

*A man who can control his tongue has knowledge,
a man of discernment keeps his temper cool.*

There are some honorable and wise proverbs as well, such as 19:18, which shows some concern about the unrelenting tone of severity and harsh discipline that is the common theme of parental advice:

*All the while there is hope, chastise your son,
but do not set out to destroy him altogether.*

I like the solid perceptiveness of 20:11:

*Even at play a child reveals
whether his actions will be pure and right.*

But that's more than offset by 22:15:

*Innate in the heart of a child is folly,
judicious beating will rid him of it.*

There are plenty of famous ones, like "Pride goes before destruction, a haughty spirit before a fall." (16:18), and lots of wonderfully silly ones like, "He who closes his eyes meditates mischief; he who purses his lips has already done wrong." (16:30)

The Holy Spirit

There is one chapter in *Proverbs*, Chapter 8, which makes some important theological assertions. Theologians and scholars have given it serious attention over the years, because it may be the origin of one of the three sides of the Trinity, the idea that God is manifest in three ways—as the Deity, as flesh and blood (Jesus), and as the Holy Spirit. This last side has many other names, depending on what religion or branch of theology you're coming from: Wisdom, the Word, Logos. But, generally speaking, the implication is that this is the *articulate* aspect of the Godhead. The Bible, then, is God speaking to us through the Holy Spirit.

Chapter 8 could be read as the Holy Spirit speaking up for itself. And guess what: *it's a woman!*

> *"I, Wisdom, am mistress of discretion,*
> *the inventor of lucidity of thought."*
> 8:12

She is almost a full partner in the act of creation:

> *"Yahweh created me when His purpose first*
> *unfolded,*
> *before the oldest of His works.*
> *From everlasting I was firmly set,*
> *from the beginning, before earth came into*
> *being...*
> *When he fixed the heavens firm, I was there...*
> *I was by His side, a master craftsman,*
> *delighting Him day after day...*
> 8:22-30

I don't see why Jewish and Christian feminists don't use this passage as proof that God is (at least partly) a woman.

Ecclesiastes

Ecclesiastes is where the Bible tackles the issue of the meaning of life. The answer? Life has no meaning. The fate of man is to die. Practically everything else is "vanity." Be prepared: you'll hear that word over and over again as you work your way through this curmudgeonly pessimistic book.

Our host is a world-weary sage named Qoheleth, who seems to take pleasure is saying things like: "All things are wearisome," (1:8) as well as "…there is nothing new under the sun." (1:9-10)

Morosely, Qoheleth sets out to test this proposition.

> *I thought to myself, "Very well, I will try pleasure and see what enjoyment has to offer."*

2:1-2

You can pretty much tell that he's not going to give it a fair shot.

> *And there it was: vanity again! This laughter, I reflected, is a madness, this pleasure no use at all.*

2:2-3

Do you trust that he really laughed? Or really had fun? Doesn't seem likely. He keeps trying, though, you've got to give him that. He observes that wealth is often thought to be a path to happiness, so he decides to give it a try. Without bothering to explain how, he becomes obscenely wealthy, builds palaces, plants vineyards, buys slaves, basically behaving like a Lotto winner. Then he steps back to assess how all this has added to his sum total of happiness. His conclusion?

> *What vanity it all is and chasing of the wind!*

2:11

There's kind of a unimaginative fumbling going on here, don't you think? As if Qoheleth were a religiously conservative exchange student brought to the United States, rigidly imitating what the American kids around him are doing, and, not succeeding in having fun, condemns the American sense of fun as meaningless. Does it occur to him that he just might not be getting it? Not a chance.

But, to be fair, Qoheleth doesn't expect us to believe that he actually did these things. *Ecclesiastes* is not a narrative but a sermon, and Qoheleth's notions of fun and nubile slave women merely philosophical abstracts. What he really wants us to understand is that life is nothing more than a meaningless interval between birth and death.

Moving along with his examination of human folly, Qoheleth decides to give wisdom a try. What he means by wisdom he doesn't say, but he doesn't have much respect for it.

> *"The fool's fate," I thought to myself, "will be my fate too. Of what use my wisdom, then? This too," I thought, "is vanity."*

2:15-16

Why Bother?

So, is it all a waste of time? Not completely, he concludes. You may as well keep busy while you're waiting to die. Working hard is not a waste of time because it gives satisfaction.

> *I see there is no happiness for man but to be happy in his work, for this is the lot assigned*

him.
3:22

It's also better to have a partner.

> *Better two than one by himself, since thus their work is really profitable. If one should fall, the other helps him up; but woe to the man by himself with no one to help him up when he falls down.*

4:9-11

Money can be useful, though seeking it can be a waste of time, since it's so easily lost and—most of all—you can't take it with you.

> *Naked from his mother's womb he came, as naked as he came he will depart again; nothing to take with him after all his efforts.*

5:14-15

The ultimate fate of man is meaningless doom.

> *Consider the work of God, who can set straight what He has made crooked? When times are prosperous, enjoy your happiness; when times are bad, consider this: the one is God's doing, as is the other, in order that man may know nothing of his destiny.*

7:13-15

"In order that man may know nothing of his destiny." Camus couldn't have put it better. Hold on a second. Let's flip this book over and look at the cover. Is this the *Bible?* Ay, caramba, it is!

The Heart of the Matter

Considering life's essential harshness and meaninglessness, Qoheleth concludes that the only reasonable thing to do is to console ourselves by leading a life of quiet hedonism.

> *Spend your life with the woman you love,*
> *through all the fleeting days of the life that God*
> *has given you under the sun; for this is the lot*
> *assigned to you in life and in the efforts you*
> *exert under the sun. Whatever work you*
> *propose to do, do it while you can, for there is*
> *neither achievement, nor planning, nor*
> *knowledge, nor wisdom in Sheol where you are*
> *going.*

8:9-10

And:

> *Rejoice in your youth, you who are young;*
> *Let your heart give you joy in your young days.*
> *Follow the promptings of your heart*
> *And the desires of your eyes.*
> 11:9

Sounds good, doesn't it? Even kind of friendly. But watch out, here comes the bucket of cold water:

> *But this you must know: for all these things*
> *God will bring you to judgment.*

11:9

The core message of *Ecclesiastes?* The universe is not fair, but God made it, so He gets to make the rules too. But don't worry, life is short, so nothing you do really matters that much.

This is in the *Bible?* What were the compilers thinking about…or smoking?

The Song of Songs

I suppose I wasn't the only high school kid who dipped into *The Song of Songs* to beef up his love poems. This book is the Bible's acknowledgement that procreation is part of life, and that lust is part of procreation.

The Song of Songs is a wedding poem in which we are invited to imagine the bride and groom speaking to each other in heated poetry. Its function is to good-naturedly overcome the strong cultural proscriptions against sensual indulgence and get everybody happily heated up for good sex.

Some of the imagery is beautiful:

> *Your lips, my promised one,*
> *distill wild honey.*
> *Honey and milk*
> *are under your tongue;*
> *and the scent of your garments*
> *is like the scent of Lebanon.*
> 4:11

Some of it is charming and funny:

> *Feed me with raisin cakes,*
> *restore me with apples,*
> *for I am sick with love*
> 2:5

Some of it is a little strange to our ears:

> ...*your hair is like a flock of goats*
> *frisking down the slopes of Gilead.*
> *Your teeth are like a flock of shorn ewes...*
> 4:1-2

And some of it is just odd:

> *To my mare harnessed to Pharaoh's chariot*
> *I compare you, my love.*
> *Your cheeks show fair between their pendants*
> *and your neck within its necklaces.*
> 1:9-11

The guy's in a chariot, looks down at his horse, and then compares what he sees with his love's *cheeks?* Maybe it reads differently in Hebrew.

Songs has a charming little plot, just enough to hang the imagery on. The bride and the bridegroom exchange praises and promises of devotion. Then the bride goes to bed, still a maiden, and the bridegroom presently comes tap-tapping at her door, expecting a night of pleasure. But she is not ready. Suddenly shy, suddenly afraid, she calls out that she has already undressed and washed her feet. Does he expect her to get out of bed and walk across that dirty floor just to let him in? What follows is the boldest passage in *Songs,* though its meaning is tastefully hidden in the imagery of the door:

My Beloved thrust his hand
through the hole in the door;
I trembled to the core of my being.
Then I rose
to open to my Beloved,

myrrh ran off my hands,
pure myrrh off my fingers,
on to the handle of the bolt.
5:4-5

A minor plot twist occurs here. By the time she gets to the door, the bridegroom has given up and left! Distraught, she dashes out in search of him, heartsick. "I sought but did not find him./ So I will rise and go through the City." (3:1-2) The bridegroom is pouting nearby, ("I went down to the nut orchard" [6:11]). Best not to over-think that.

Presently she finds him, and together they go on a night of wild wandering through the fields and vineyards. Then there is a tasteful pause…and they wake up under the same apple tree where her mother conceived her. Wow. What could have happened?

The Book of Isaiah

The Book of Isaiah is huge, both in length and in its towering influence in the formation of fundamental Christian concepts. It's full of great poetry, great bluster, and thundering prophecies pregnant with meaning even today.

Scholars believe that *The Book of Isaiah* is comprised of the writings of three authors, contributing to the text over a period of about two hundred years. That accounts for some of its eerie dead-on prophecies—because some of the time the writer was prophesying backwards.

Out of *Isaiah* comes the idea of a Messiah. Out of *Isaiah* comes Hell (and a hint of Heaven). Out of *Isaiah* comes Satan. Out of *Isaiah* comes eternal damnation. Out of *Isaiah* comes the idea that God will preserve a holy remnant of humanity from destruction. Out of *Isaiah* comes this:

> *...the maiden is with child*
> *and will soon give birth to a son*
> *whom she will call Immanuel.*
> 7:14

See what I'm saying? Out of *Isaiah* come the parts for assembling the whole haunted house of Christianity.

Isaiah was a preacher of such mind-warping power that he had political influence as well as spiritual authority. Think of Billy Graham times ten. He advised four Judean kings on, among other things, how to deal with three Assyrian assaults on Jerusalem. And he did a good job—especially with the last one in 701 BCE, where he advised the king that if he did nothing but rely on Yahweh the Assyrians would go away. And they did! (Even the Assyrians admit that in their own records, though they maintained they had to withdraw because they were being attacked by the Babylonians on another front. But never mind. Isaiah called it, and he gets the credit.)

That was just his political career. In the realm of prophecy, his specialty, Isaiah was second to none, spewing forth terrifying visions of Jerusalem's destruction, visions that in some cases were so shattering that they seem to transcend history and speak about things that were never before imagined.

Hang gliding
There's no way we're going to be able to wrap our minds around *The Book of Isaiah* in a single essay. Instead we're going to strap ourselves into a hang glider and float over the terrain of Judah, dipping down when we see something interesting.

We're in the early 700s BCE. Up to the north you can make out Samaria, where the other ten Israelite tribes live; a dark and smoky land far gone into paganism and human sacrifice. North of them you can see the glinting spears of the Assyrian army, as it prepares to conquer them. Soon that army will be headed this way.

Directly below us you can see the citizens of Jerusalem, drinking and partying, cheating one another in business, abusing the poor, worshipping their little pagan gods, and paying only lip service to Yahweh, who is losing His patience with them. If you look closer, you can see a man walking around naked. That's Isaiah, dramatizing how the Assyrians treat their captives, warning the people that's what is going to happen to them if they don't renew their faith. He walks around like that for three years, but nobody seems to pay attention.

He has a special warning for the women of the day that's worth looking at. It gives you a taste of Isaiah's gift for scalding, disturbing images:

Yahweh said: "Because of the haughtiness
of the daughters of Zion,
the way they walk with their heads held high
and enticing eyes,
the way they mince along,
tinkling the bangles on their feet,
the Lord will give the daughters of Zion itching heads
and uncover their nakedness. ...

Instead of scent, a stink;
instead of belt, a rope;
instead of hair elaborately done, a shaven scalp,
and instead of gorgeous dress, a sack;
and brand marks instead of beauty."
3:16-24

What these people don't understand, what Isaiah is trying to warn them about, is that their God is abandoning them. In Chapter 6 Yahweh makes the official announcement: the Jews are a dead people walking.

> *"There will be a great emptiness in the country*
> *And, though a tenth of the people remain,*
> *it will be stripped like a terebinth*[13]
> ~~of which, once felled,~~ *only the stock remains.*

[13] A type of tree found in the western Mediterranean area.

> *The stock is a holy seed.*
6:12-13

They're done for, headed for defeat, capture, and slavery. Yahweh does relent a little at the last moment, promising to save a few of the people as a "holy seed" for a new generation of Jews that maybe, finally, will get it right. Later on this group will be known as the remnant, though there's no way to tell who's in that exclusive club.

From this pronouncement it's only a hop, skip, and a jump to bumper stickers warning you that the driver of the car in front of you may be "raptured" at any moment, rapture being fundamentalist Christian code for the moment that God will sweep up His holy remnant to heaven as the end of days approaches. We have Isaiah to thank for this.

A Glowing Future Awaits Them

Now that Yahweh has served His divorce papers, half of Isaiah's job is to terrify the people with moaning prophecies illustrating how horrific their fate will be. But they're not that easy to scare, probably because they've drifted so far away from the true path, partly because they've heard these threats so many times. One of the kings that consults Isaiah, Hezekiah, learns that the doom that awaits his people will fall on the next generation, not his:

> *Then Isaiah said to Hezekiah... "Sons sprung from you, sons begotten by you, will be chosen to be eunuchs in the palace of the king of Babylon."*
>
> *Hezekiah said to Isaiah, "This word of Yahweh that you announce is reassuring," for he was*

> *thinking, "There is going to be peace and
> security during my own lifetime."*

39:5-8

'Whew!' he's thinking. 'At least it ain't happening to *me*, you know what I'm saying?'

Pageant of Prophecies
Let's take a look at how Isaiah lays out the basic elements of what will become Christian eschatology. Pay attention as we tick off the concepts he introduces, concepts that today are part of the mental furniture of just about everyone living in the Western world. Let's start with Hell.

Up until now, of course, there's been no afterlife of any kind. There's only Sheol, the refrigerated warehouse of all the dead, good and evil alike. That's about to change. Just outside the walls of Jerusalem, to the southwest, likes a narrow ravine known as the Valley of Ben-Hinnom, a name which is often abbreviated to Gehenna. During times of faithfulness to Yahweh, Gehenna was merely the city dump. Offal, parts of animals prohibited from consumption, junk left over after sacrifices—all was tossed into the valley to be burnt. During the frequent lapses from faithfulness to Yahweh, human sacrifices were carried out in the valley. One of Gehenna's other names was Topheth, after the drums that were banged on to cover the screams of the victims. That's all anybody knew about Gehenna until Isaiah, reaching down for a really memorable image for how the Assyrians will be punished for oppressing the Jews, comes up with this:

> *For in Topheth there has been prepared
> beforehand,
> Yes, made ready for Molech*[14]

> *a pit deep and wide*
> *with straw and wood in plenty.*
> *The breath of Yahweh, like a stream of*
> *brimstone,*
> *will set fire to it.*
> 30:33

Later, Isaiah says this:

> *Which of us can live with this devouring fire,*
> *which of us exist in everlasting flames?*
> 33:14

And later, he rounds out the horror with this:

> *Their worm will not die*
> *nor their fire go out...*
> 66:24

There it is: Hell. Welcome to our culture, O noble concept!

Even today the word "Gehenna" is a synonym for Hell, especially in fundamentalist Christian circles. Jesus uses the word eleven times in the Gospels to describe a place where both body and soul can be destroyed.

Isaiah goes on to flesh out the portrait of Hell a little more. He provides a good introductory topography in Chapter 34, even installing the first demon in the person of Lilith, a creature from Jewish lore that attacked children.

---

[14] Molech was a pagan deity who was best appeased by having children sacrificed to him.

As for Satan, he's introduced in Chapter 14, when, in describing what is going to happen to the king of Babylon, Isaiah says this:

> *How did you come to fall from the heavens,*
> *Daystar, son of Dawn?*
> *How did you come to be thrown to the ground,*
> *you who enslaved the nations?*
> *You who used to think to yourself,*
> *"I will climb up to the heavens;*
> *and higher than the stars of God*
> *I will set my throne...."*
> *What! Now you have fallen to Sheol,*
> *to the very bottom of the abyss.*

14:12-15

"Daystar" is the planet Venus, which often appears to fall below the horizon. The Latin translation of the Hebrew word for Daystar is Lucifer. Lucifer is one of the Christian names for Satan.

Your Dead Will Come to Life

Okay, we have Hell. How about the Resurrection? In a hymn celebrating the eventual return to Jerusalem and the reunion of the Jews with their God (at least the holy remnant), Isaiah says this:

> *Your dead will come to life*
> *their corpses will rise;*
> *awake, exult,*
> *all you who lie in the dust,*
> *for your dew is a radiant dew*
> *and the land of ghosts will give birth.*
> 26:19

Suddenly, immortality is within reach.

The Messiah

Let's look at the relevant verse again:

> *...the maiden is with child*
> *and will soon give birth to a son*
> *whom she will call Immanuel*

7:14

"The *maiden* with child." On the face of it, that's just plain scary. Does he really mean a *virgin?* How could he have possibly have known? Scholars have wrung their hands over this question for generations. The Hebrew noun probably used here, "almah," means merely "a young woman of child bearing age who has not yet had a child." So "almah" denotes a woman who is *probably* a virgin, though the word doesn't specify virginity. In the Greek translation of the Old Testament (which is the oldest text we have) the word used is "parthenos," which unequivocally means "virgin."

As far back as the early sixteenth century theologians were scuffling with each other on this question. Martin Luther offered a prize of 100 gulden to any Jewish scholar who could find an instance in the Old Testament where the word "almah" does *not* mean a virgin. Like Christians before and after him, Luther flatly believed that this verse was a prophecy of the Virgin Mary.

The name "Immanuel" is almost as controversial. Christians use the name Immanuel as one of the names of Jesus, but for the Jews it merely means "God with us." Isaiah probably wasn't referring to Jesus specifically when he used this name. Or, you never know, maybe he was. As a prophet, Isaiah has no equal. The simplest interpretation is that he *probably* was thinking of a Messiah, but not in the Christian sense as the son of God; more like a coming of a charismatic leader like King David who will restore the Jews to their rightful place as history's Chosen People.

But the Christians aren't satisfied with that. They want the Messiah to be more than just the return of a great king, and *Isaiah* gives them plenty of clues to support that belief. Chapter 53 is just jaw dropping in its prophetic power and specificity. The figure Isaiah is describing he calls "the servant," and these lines are about his suffering:

> *...a man of sorrows and familiar with suffering,*
> *a man to make people screen their faces;*
> *he was despised and we took no account of*
> *him.*
>
> *And yet ours were the sufferings he bore,*
> *ours the sorrows he carried.*
> *But we, we thought of him as someone*
> *punished,*
> *struck by God and brought low.*
> *Yet he was pierced through for our faults,*
> *crushed for our sins.*
> *On him lies a punishment that brings us peace,*
> *and through his wounds we are healed.*

53:3-5

Let's pause for a second to inventory what this quotation contains. This man is suffering, yet "ours were the sufferings he bore." He is "pierced through for our faults," and "through his wounds we are healed." Onward:

> *By force and by law he was taken;*
> *would anyone plead his cause?*
> *Yes, he was torn away from the land of the*

> *living;*
> *for our faults struck down in death.*
> *They gave him a grave with the wicked,*
> *a tomb with the rich,*
> *though he had done no wrong*
> *and there had been no perjury in his mouth.*
> *Yahweh has been pleased to crush him with*
> *suffering.*
> *If he offers his life in atonement,*
> *he shall see his heirs, he shall have a long life*
> *and through him what Yahweh wishes will be*
> *done.*

53:8-10

"…for our faults struck down in death…he offers his life in atonement…" It's almost too right on, but as far as I know, nobody's claiming this was written after the fact. A copy of *Isaiah* was found among the Dead Sea Scrolls, which are dated no later than 70 BCE, that is, *before* the birth of Jesus. So, no possibility of backwards prophesying here.

What's left? Oh, Heaven. There's not much, just a blurry reference in Chapter 35 to a "redeemed" people living in an idyllic land in a state of "everlasting joy." Of course it's only Isaiah talking about the return from exile, but remember, it's his rhetorical excesses that we have inherited as Christian doctrine.

Homicidal Trance and the Apocalypse
Beyond his prophetic gifts, Isaiah was a consummate terrifying meltdown preacher. When he really gets up to speed, the roiling of words that come out of his divine mania can go almost anywhere. There is a passage known as "the vengeance of Yahweh" that was written in a mood of mass-murdering exultation. It's in the form

of an interview with Yahweh:

> *–Why are your garments red,*
> *your clothes as if you had trodden the*
> *winepress?*
>
> *–I have trodden the winepress alone....*
> *In my anger I trod them down,*
> *trampled them in my wrath.*
> *Their juice spattered my garments,*
> *and all my clothes are stained....*
> *I crushed the people in my fury,*
> *trampled them in my anger,*
> *and made the juice of them run all over the*
> *ground.*

63:3-6

Anyone hearing a popular song here? How about: ♪"He is trampling out the vintage where grapes of wrath are stored…"♪

This crime scene segues pretty naturally into the imagery that people associate with the Apocalypse, the beginning of the end that is the subject of *Revelations,* the last book in the Bible. Here, as with so much, it seems to be prefigured in *Isaiah*:

> *For see how Yahweh comes in fire,*
> *His chariots like the tempest,*
> *to assuage his anger with burning,*
> *His threats with flaming fire.*
>
> *For by fire will Yahweh execute judgment,*
> *and by sword, against all mankind.*
> *The victims of Yahweh will be many…*

Their worm will not die,
Nor their fire go out;
They will be loathsome to all mankind.
66:15-16

"Their worm will not die" means maggots will eat the bodies of the damned forever. The man knew how to throw down horrific images, didn't he?

Without *The Book of Isaiah* to glean from, Christianity would have had to invent its core beliefs.

Jeremiah

The prophet Jeremiah was an eye witness to the Babylonian conquest of Judah and the deportation of its people at the beginning of the fifth century BCE. He's the original guy wearing the sandwich board warning "Repent, for the End is Near!" Shaking with rage, exasperated beyond endurance, Jeremiah did everything he could to awake the Jewish community to its imminent danger, all the time knowing his efforts were futile. How did he know they were futile? Because Yahweh told him so. But He told Jeremiah to issue the warnings anyway, so the people would have no excuse later.

How do you win with a God like that?

Jeremiah is the source of the word "jeremiad," which means an angry lament filled with dire predictions. That tone is probably why Jeremiah was so hated in his own time: the red-veined face with popping eyes pushing into yours, shouting "You're going to be sorry! You're going to sorry!" and "I told you so! I told you so!" Kings tried to kill him, priests locked him up in an underground cell, and a group of prominent citizens dropped him into a cistern. But he never shut up.

The text itself is a confused and repetitive jumble of prophecies, poems, and diatribes stuck together with little sense of chronological or narrative order. Jeremiah seems basically to have lined up his indignations like clay pigeons and let fly with a double load of bitter invective. But let's try to make some sense of it.

"You bastard vine"
The first twenty-five chapters of *Jeremiah* are prophecies of

impending doom for Jerusalem. It's inspired ranting. Like a tireless tag team, Jeremiah and Yahweh together heap threats and invective on the hapless people of Israel and Judah alike. In a hysterical trance, Jeremiah goes on for page after page. It's hypnotic. He never quite repeats himself; new images seethe up as if from an inexhaustible cauldron of murderous rage. Much of it is uttered by Yahweh through Jeremiah's mouth, and He is not happy:

> *"Yet I had planted, a choice vine,*
> *a shoot of soundest stock.*
> *How is it now that you have become a*
> *degenerate plant,*
> *you bastard vine?"*
> 2:21

Jeremiah sees what's in store for his people:

> *I am in anguish! I writhe with pain!*
> *Walls of my heart!*
> *My heart is throbbing!*
> *I cannot keep quiet,*
> *for I have heard the trumpet call*
> *and the cry of war.*
> 4:19

It's time to pay for worshipping pagan gods. Yahweh speaks:

> *I will also pull your skirts up as high as your*
> *face*
> *and let your shame be seen.*
> *Oh! Your adulteries, your shrieks of pleasure,*
> *your vile prostitution!*

13:26-27

John Calvin couldn't have said it better.

Getting Back at Them
Jeremiah isn't insensitive to the loathing of his enemies, and he isn't above being small-minded and vindictive. He actually tries to sic Yahweh on them.

> *Listen to me, Yahweh,*
> *hear what my adversaries are saying. ...*
> *They are digging a pit for me ...*
> *hand their sons over to famine,*
> *abandon them to the edge of the sword.*
> *May their wives become*
> *childless and widowed.*
> *May their husbands die of plague. ...*
> *Keep their destruction always in mind,*
> *when the time for your anger comes, deal with*
> *them.*
> 18:19-23

Unbelievable, isn't it? He's practically ordering Yahweh to take time out from managing the universe to go after his personal hit list. Even if Jeremiah is one of the major prophets, even if he's an eye-witness to the lowest moment in Jewish history, even if he has Yahweh's support, you just want to *squash* him.

That Impossible Little Man
In Chapter 38 the city fathers come after Jeremiah. By now they are aware that the Babylonians are approaching. They're on edge, uncertain what to do. Jeremiah's cries of doom are becoming more shrill and maddening. Have you ever tried to think when

someone's screaming in your face? Finally the leaders have had enough. They go before the king demanding that he do something to shut Jeremiah up:

> *"Let this man be put to death; he is unquestionably disheartening the remaining soldiers in the city, and all the people too, by talking like this. The fellow does not have the welfare of this people at heart so much as its ruin."*
> 38:4-5

King Zedekiah, whose indecisive nature will cost him dearly in the end, answers that he's not inclined to protect Jeremiah, and that's good enough for the leaders—they seize Jeremiah and throw him into a well that's nearly dry, "and into the mud Jeremiah sank." (38:6)

As is typical of this king, Zedekiah changes his mind. He orders the eunuch Ebed-melech to pull Jeremiah out of the well. What happens next is priceless. Ebed-melech gets a bunch of rags out of a storehouse. He lowers the rags down to Jeremiah, telling him they are "for you to put under your armpits to pad the ropes." (38:12-13) What an incredible detail! Think about it. Twenty-six hundred years ago a man gave another man a handful of rags to protect his armpits. And it's in the Bible!

Soon after, Nebuchadnezzar, the king of Babylon, lays siege to Jerusalem and the city quickly succumbs. Poor King Zedekiah flees through his garden gate and is promptly captured. Nebuchadnezzar has Zedekiah's sons put to death in front of his eyes, and then had his eyes put out. Then, "…loading him with chains, carried him off to Babylon" to be a living trophy of

Nebuchadnezzar's great victory. (39:8)

Zion

Now that the worst has happened, Jeremiah's tone softens a bit. He issues morale-boosting prophecies to assure his people that they will not be exiled forever. He promises that seventy years hence they'll be allowed to return (which they did; Cyrus the Great, conqueror of Babylon, released the exiles in 538 BCE).

Jeremiah uses the word "Zion," which originally meant "fortress of David," to symbolize the promise of return:

> *In those days and at that time*
> *the sons of Israel will return;*
> *they will come weeping*
> *in search of Yahweh their God.*
> *They will ask the way to Zion,*
> *Their faces will turn in that direction...*

50:4-5

The late nineteenth century Zionist movement, composed mainly of European Jews who advocated the return of Jews around the world to their ancestral homeland, took its inspiration in part from the prophecies of Jeremiah.

Israel? Judah?

Let's clear up a little problem of nomenclature. The names used to identify the Chosen People and the Promised Land slip around a bit over the course of their history. First there was Abraham, who led a group of people known as Hebrews. Abraham's grandson was Jacob, whom God renamed Israel. Israel in turn had twelve sons who were the patriarchs of the twelve tribes that conquered the Promised Land, which they called Israel. After the civil wars at the end of Solomon's reign, ten of these tribes formed a separate kingdom, keeping the name Israel. The southern lands were controlled by the tribe of Judah. Its occupants were called Jews. The focus of the Old Testament is the history of the Jews.

The Assyrian conquest of Israel in 721 BCE absorbed that kingdom and forever dispersed the ten tribes. The Babylonian conquest of Judah in 587 BCE resulted in the scattering of its people—mostly to Babylon.

When the Jews were allowed to return to their homeland in 538 BCE, it once again was called Judah (or Judea), though it now included much of the area to the north once called Israel. Today the land that was once called Judah is called Israel, though its citizens are still referred to as Jews.

It's confusing.

A New Covenant
Covenants are major contracts between Yahweh and His Chosen People. They're rare, and when a new one is announced it's a big deal. The First Covenant was promulgated just after the Flood, when Yahweh promised Noah that never again would He "strike down every living thing as I have done." (Gen. 8:21) The Second Covenant was Yahweh's promise to Abraham that he would be "the father of a multitude of nations." (Gen. 17:4) It also placed a great deal emphasis on the importance of circumcision. (You may remember that Moses had to take a remedial course on that one, much to his discomfort. [4:24])

The covenant announced in *Jeremiah* sets forth an important shift in how Yahweh will to make Himself known to man. From now on, He says, He intends to plant Himself within the individual hearts of His believers. Here's how He puts it:

> *Deep within them I will plant my Law, writing it on their hearts. Then I will be their God and they shall be my people. There will be no further need for neighbor to try to teach neighbor, or brother to say to brother, "Learn to know Yahweh!" No, they will all know me, the least no less than the greatest. It is Yahweh who speaks.*
> 31:33-34

If you didn't notice, that pretty much puts priests out of work. Needless to say, that covenant was quietly shelved. But it's in the record, and doubtless Martin Luther was aware of it when he fired the priests again in 1517 CE.

So now we are at the same moment in Jewish history that we were at the end of *II Kings*. That is, we're at the very bottom. The northern kingdom of Israel has been gone for over 130 years, utterly destroyed, its people scattered, never to be heard from again.[15] Now it's 587 BCE, and it's Judah's turn to be dismantled. Off to Babylon with you, off to Egypt. Everyone except the old, the infirm, and the mentally challenged has been deported. Jerusalem is in ruins, an expanse of smoking rubble, a place where old people pick at trash heaps and swing their crutches at bony dogs.

---

[15] The Mormons beg to differ. They believe they're the spiritual descendents of the ten lost tribes of Israel.

Lamentations

Lamentations is a collection of five formal dirges expressing the Jewish community's grief over the destruction of the Temple in Jerusalem in 587 BCE It is recited each year on August 9, the date traditionally assigned to the Babylonian sacking of the city.

This is not meant to be spontaneous grief. The structure is very formal. Four of the dirges are acrostics—each line beginning with a different letter of the Hebrew alphabet. The fifth is not an acrostic, but has twenty-two verses like the rest.

The way the Babylonians won this little war was to lay siege to Jerusalem, and wait until the city buckled to its knees. The second dirge describes what it was like inside:

> *My eyes wasted away with weeping*
> *my entrails shuddered,*
> *my liver spilled on the ground*
> *at the ruin of the daughters of my people,*
> *as children, mere infants, fainted*
> *in the squares of the Citadel.*
> 2:11

It got worse than that:

> *With their own hands, tenderhearted women*
> *have boiled their children;*
> *these have been their food*
> *in the disaster that fell on the daughter of my*
> *people.*
> 4:10

We've run into this image before—mothers eating their own children during a time of war—in *Deuteronomy* 28. The horror it conveys is unbearable.

It's interesting that little mention is made of the Babylonians. That's probably because, from the Jewish point-of-view, they weren't important. They were merely the tool an embittered and disillusioned Yahweh was using to crush this faithless people. The fact that they still pray to Him after they've lost everything is, I suppose, proof that they aren't so faithless after all. Whether that's enough for Yahweh to change His mind and take them back isn't clear.

For the Jews, history is how Yahweh expresses His feelings, and history hasn't been kind to them.

Ezekiel

Get ready to put on your sunglasses. When Ezekiel touches off one of his visions, the spouting fires, blinding colors, booming sounds and strange spinning figures are as spectacular as a Super Bowl half-time.

There is a good reason for this: Ezekiel's audience is no longer in Judah, and neither is he. Ezekiel is preaching to the community of exiles that are now probably living in a Jewish ghetto in downtown Babylon. His first job is to get their attention; his second, to remind them of their special status as Jews, God's Chosen People. There's a real danger here of them forgetting that. Now that they're no longer living in the Promised Land, it would only be natural for them to assimilate into Babylonian society. Ezekiel's job is to keep that from happening. To do that he has to startle, fascinate and frighten his people with visions of their past, present and future.

Chariot of Yahweh
Of course, the narrative doesn't just come out announce this strategy. And to be fair to Ezekiel, he doesn't seem to be aware of it himself. He's anything but a coolly calculating man. There is a rapturous, horrifying quality to his visionary encounters with Yahweh that suggest a frightened child being abused by a wild adult, or an Iowa farmer recounting his flying saucer ride. *Ezekiel* begins with one of the most bizarre visions, called the "Chariot of Yahweh." The overall impression is like walking down a carnival midway on LSD. Here's a paraphrase of the vision (or just read Chapter 1 yourself):

> *Ezekiel is standing on a river bank and*

> *suddenly he sees four fierce sphinx-like creatures, each with four wings and four faces, prancing about in a stormy sky, their wings touching. Balls of fire dart between the animals. Bolts of lightning are snapping everywhere. Beside each of the sphinxes is a wheel, and also somehow the wheels are concentric, and along the rims of the wheels are (yech!) eyes. Above the sphinxes is a crystalline vault, and on top of the vault is a sapphire throne. Sitting on the throne, surrounded by rainbows, is a flaming man. Ezekiel realizes he's in the presence of Yahweh.*

Yahweh sends Ezekiel on a seven-day retreat to the camp of some exiles living beside the river Chebar. There Yahweh tells Ezekiel that "I have appointed you as sentry to the House of Israel." (3:17) Then, as if to make his job impossible, Yahweh strikes him dumb and makes him into a mime. Ezekiel returns to the Jewish ghetto.

Sand Castles

Specifically, Ezekiel's job is to make himself into a living theater of what's happening in Jerusalem, which has not fallen yet.[16] Yahweh instructs him to make a brick model of Jerusalem:

> *You are then to besiege it, trench around it, ~~build earthworks, pitch~~ camps and bring up*

---

[16] History tells us that the exile to Babylonia took place over the course of three deportations over a period of fifteen years, beginning in 597 BCE (the big one is the one in 587 BCE, when Jerusalem fell). At the time Ezekiel was living in Babylon Jerusalem had not fallen yet.

> *battering rams all around. Then take up an
> iron pan and place it as if it were an iron wall
> between you and the city. ...* [You] *are besieging
> it.*
> 4:1-3

It just gets more and more bizarre. To dramatize what's going on in Jerusalem, Yahweh tells Ezekiel to lie down and fast for 230 days. Finally, when the time is up, for breakfast Ezekiel is allowed to eat only barley cakes cooked over dried human shit.

Hold on. That's a little much even for Ezekiel, who reminds Yahweh that he is a very clean man. Yahweh relents and switches the cooking fuel to cow's dung. (4:14-16) What a moment! A man and his Creator arguing over what kind of shit to cook food over!

So Ezekiel lies there like a one-man wire service. The exiles come to his bed from time to time to catch up with what's going on in Jerusalem. Periodically Yahweh lets Ezekiel speak, if you can call the curses and lamentations that stream forth speaking.

The truth is, the relationship between Yahweh and his people has never been a healthy one. Right from the beginning, with the flood in *Genesis 7*, Yahweh has wanted to wipe out this stubborn and faithless people. It's like a bad marriage that somehow manages to go on and on, slowly deteriorating until things are just plain rotten, both sides loathing each other. Listen to Yahweh now:

> *Finished! The end is coming.... Now disaster
> is going to follow on disaster. The end is
> coming, the end is coming for you.... Soon I am
> going to pour out my fury on you and exhaust*

> *my anger at on you…and call you to account for your filthy practices…. And so you will learn that I am Yahweh, and that I strike.*
> 7:2-9

You can almost see the spittle flying as this God paces back and forth in a homicidal rage. As if to prove His point Yahweh seizes Ezekiel by the hair and whisks him over the desert to Jerusalem and takes him inside the Temple to show him the filthy practices going on in there. It's what you would expect: it's smoky inside and everybody is bowing to idols. There's even one mystery abomination. "Look at them now," says Yahweh, "putting that branch to their nostrils." (8:18)

Your guess is as good as mine as to what the branch was or why you would want to put it to your nostrils.

Free Will

The rest of *Ezekiel* is mainly imaginative ranting, but a few passages are worth noting.

For example, the editors still haven't come to grips with the issue of free will, though they keep bringing up.

> *I even gave them laws that were not good and observances by which they could never live; and I polluted them with their own offerings, made them sacrifice all their first-born; which was to punish them, so that they would learn that I am Yahweh.*
> 20:25-26

'If I make you misbehave it's still your fault.' How unfair can you get? How can that *not* make you crazy?

Big-Membered Egyptians

Chapter 16 is a curiosity unto itself. It's supposed to be an allegorical history of Israel, in which the nation is represented as a girl growing up under the care of a loving but severe uncle-figure. But the story quickly spirals out of control. The hot haze of pornography begins to seep up through the words.

> *Your breasts and your hair both grew, but you were quite naked. Then I saw you as you were passing. Your time had come, the time for love. I spread part of my cloak over you and covered your nakedness...and you became mine. I bathed you in water,...I anointed you with oil.*
> 16:7-10

You can almost smell the acid sweat of the uncle's lust. He goes on to dress her in lavish clothing, and bedeck her in jewelry.

> *"You grew more and more beautiful; and you rose to be queen."*
> 16:13-14

Then what happens? She becomes a prostitute and an idolatress!

> *You have lain down for those big-membered neighbors, the Egyptians...*
> 16:26

Yes, in those days it was the Egyptians who were legendarily hung. But what's worse than laying down for an Egyptian is that the queen, unlike a real working girl, doesn't accept payment; instead she pays *them!* On top of everything, *she's losing money!* That's the last straw.

> *I'm going to band together all the lovers who have pleasured you.... I will strip you in front of them, and let them see you naked.... They will then whip up the crowd against you; you will be stoned and run through with a sword...*
> 16:37-40

Kind of a tough love deal, I guess. Don't worry, they make up.

Later on, in Chapter 23, she's at it again:

> *She flaunted her whoring, she stripped naked.... She began whoring worse than ever, remembering her girlhood, when she had played the whore in the land of Egypt, when she had been infatuated by profligates big-membered as donkeys, ejaculating as violently as stallions.*
> 23:19-20

This is the pornography of Bible-pounding preachers, damning the behavior it excites them to think about.

Fathers and Sons

In Chapter 18 Yahweh takes a well-worn proverb out of commission. Here it is:

> *The fathers have eaten unripe grapes; and the children's teeth are set on edge?*
> 18:2

Here's what Yahweh has to say about it:

> *"As I live—it is the Lord Yahweh who speaks—*

> *there will no longer be any reason to repeat this proverb in Israel. See now: all life belongs to me; the father's life and the son's life, both alike belong to me. The man who has sinned, he is the one who shall die."*
> 18:3-4

In other words, sons no longer have to pay for the sins of their fathers. Each person is responsible for his own behavior. Almost in spite of itself, the Bible is growing up.

Resurrection and Return

Here it is, as direct and explicit as you could possibly want. The promise of an afterlife is now part of the record. It occurs in Chapter 37 in the famous passage about the valley of bones. Yahweh takes Ezekiel there and gives him the privilege of making the bones come back to life.

> *While I was prophesying, there was a noise, a sound of clattering; and the bones joined together. I looked and saw that they were covered with sinew; flesh was growing on them and skin was covering them...they came to life again and stood up on their feet, a great, an immense army.*
> 37:7-10

Yahweh explains that "these bones are the whole House of Israel." He tells Ezekiel to go back to the exiles and give them this message:

> *The Lord Yahweh says this: I am now going to open your graves; I mean to raise you from*

> *your graves, my people, and lead you back to*
> *the soil of Israel.*
> 37:12-13

The exiles now have every reason to hope that the time for returning home is not far away. A very good sign is that the last eight chapters of *Ezekiel* are almost entirely devoted to plan specifications for the re-building of the Temple in Jerusalem. You wouldn't be talking about re-building unless you were about to go there, would you?

Daniel

Daniel is the first all-out apocalyptic book of the Bible, prophesying a cataclysmic end-of-time event. Composed in the mid-second century BCE, *Daniel* was one of the last books to get in before the Old Testament closed up shop. By then Judah was part of the Greek Empire, and the Jews were expected to adopt Hellenistic religious practices. If you were a Jewish religious writer defending your faith, you had to be careful. So parts of *Daniel* are written in a kind of code, in which the numbers and symbols carry meaning that only rabbis could decipher.

Chapters 2-6 recount the adventures of Daniel in the courts of several Babylonian kings, starting with Nebuchadnezzar, who, you'll remember, sacked Jerusalem in 587 BCE. Daniel is part of a group of bright boys who are being groomed to become advisors to the king, and his adventures at the court form the first few chapters. The writing style is simple, as if pitched to a less-educated or younger audience.

They're good stories, but I don't see the point of re-telling them. They mainly involve Daniel interpreting dreams that baffle the king's pagan sages. These dreams, of course, affirm the supremacy of Yahweh among all the gods worshipped by the Babylonians. In another adventure, three of Daniel's Jewish friends are thrown into a furnace because they won't worship the Babylonian god. They emerge unharmed. In the best story, Daniel, the target of a court intrigue, is thrown into a lion's den. He spends the night, emerges unharmed, and his enemies are thrown in instead. They don't even reach the floor before the lions "crushed their bones to pieces." (6:24)

I Have a Dream

In Chapter 7 Daniel begins to have his own dreams, and that brings in the apocalyptic stuff, some of which is important, some just weirdly interesting.

In the first dream (Chapter 7), Daniel sees four fantastic beasts: a lion with wings; a bear with ribs in its mouth (as if suddenly summoned from a meal); a winged leopard with four heads; and an absolutely terrifying mystery animal with ten horns and huge iron teeth. The four animals represent the four empires that have, one after the other, conquered Judah: the Babylonians, the Medes (a subset of the Babylonians), the Persians, and the Greeks. In the dream all four are defeated, with the mystery animal (the Greeks) wholly destroyed.

The important part of the dream comes when the Kingdom of Heaven descends to clean up this pagan mess. As in *Ezekiel*, an old man surrounded by flames takes his seat on a flaming throne with flaming wheels. We can safely assume this is Yahweh. Here's the key passage (Daniel is speaking):

> *I gazed into the vision of the night,*
> *and I saw, coming on the clouds of heaven,*
> *one like a son of man.*
> *He came to the one of great age*
> *and was led into his presence.*
> *On him was conferred sovereignty...*
> 7:12

For Jews, this is a prophecy of the Messiah, the next King David. For Christians, it is a prophecy of Jesus. In the New Testament, Matthew cites this passage as proof that Jesus is the "son of man" mentioned in Daniel's vision.

The dream ends in a hail of hallucinogenic arithmetic (ten kings, plus one king, minus three kings, one of which rules for "a time, two times, and a half a time"). These are the sort of math problems you get when you stay up too late doing your homework.

In the second dream (Chapter 8) a one-horned goat (Alexander the Great) demolishes a two-horned ram (the combined empires of the Medes and the Persians). Later, the goat's single horn breaks into four smaller ones (symbolizing the dividing of Alexander's empire into four smaller kingdoms after his death).

The third dream revolves around a deft recalculation of when Jerusalem will be rebuilt. The problem is that the deadline for Jeremiah's original prediction of seventy years after the Babylonian conquest passed several centuries ago. So the angel Gabriel appears before Daniel to explain how math is done in heaven. 'It wasn't supposed to be *seventy* years," the angel says, 'it was supposed to be seventy *weeks* of years. No, actually,' the angel continues, tapping on his flaming sapphire calculator, 'it's sixty-two weeks plus seven weeks plus one-and-a-half weeks.'

So the final number is seventy and one-half weeks of years, or 493.5 years. That calculation just *happens* to get us to the historical period that the author of *Daniel* is writing in! Wow! How about that? At the Heavenly Mathematics Institute, you do the problem over and over until you get the answer you want.

The Great Vision
This is the big one. Here we're going to get the Resurrection as a final package.

The vision begins with an impenetrable review of the future ravages of the Promised Land by foreign kings. When the last king is finally brought down, Daniel promises, things are going to get really dramatic. It's the beginning of the end:

> *There is going to be a time of great distress, unparalleled since nations first came into existence. When that time comes, your own people will be spared, all those whose names are found written in the Book. Of those who lie sleeping in the dust of the earth many will awake, some to everlasting life, some to shame and everlasting disgrace.*
> 12:1-3

The Resurrection was introduced in *Ezekiel* 37, but see what's been added here? *Judgment!* Everlasting life for some, everlasting disgrace for others.

Daniel ends with three more children's stories, one of them R rated. Two old judges become inflamed with lust over a virtuous beauty named Susanna. Together, they plot to rape her. One hot day she decides to take a bath under a tree in her private garden. The old judges decide this is their chance. They burst into the garden and shamelessly confront her.

> *"We want to have you, so give in and let us! Refuse, and we will both give evidence that a young man was with you and that was why you sent your maids away."*

13:20-21

Susanna knows she is trapped. If she says yes, she loses her virtue. If she says no, she will be put to death because no one is going to take her word over that of the judges. So she starts screaming, and the old men start screaming too. At a town meeting the next day the old men give their testimony against her, and without further ado the town folk prepare to put her to death. Only, guess what? Young Daniel is there to save the day! He demands a chance to defend the woman. He arranges to interview the old judges separately, and asks them each which kind of tree was the woman bathing under. They have no idea, of course; after all they were watching a naked girl taking a bath. Who *cares* about what kind of tree she was under? But Daniel makes them guess anyway. One judge says a mastic tree, the other an oak tree. They're both wrong, and thus both are proven to be liars. For this they are put to death instead of the virtuous woman. By the way, the text doesn't tell us what kind of tree it really was, or even if there was a tree at all.

Slowly the pieces of the Christian package are being assembled. The Messiah has been strongly hinted at. The Resurrection is almost done. Judgment is in its formative stages. Hell is coming along. Heaven hasn't really gotten much attention yet, but it's on its way, don't worry.

The Minor Prophets

They probably didn't think they were minor, and the criteria for getting promoted to the majors aren't clear, but if you read them you can kind of get a feel for it. Their proclamations sound less like thunder than like children playing with pots and pans.

Hosea

Hosea was a contemporary of the great prophet Isaiah. His job was to ring the alarm to the northern kingdom of Israel that the Assyrians were about to devour them. His method was performance art, a self-inflicted morality play. He takes a temple prostitute for his wife, "for the country itself has become nothing but a whore." (1:2) They have three children, to whom he gives hateful names—Jezreel (the site of a famous massacre), Unloved, and No-People-of –Mine—to dramatize Yahweh's disgust. Not fair to the kids, though.

Then Hosea, in a storm of pious rage, throws his wife out. Then he takes her back. This is supposed to mirror Yahweh's relationship with his people; first righteous anger (you whore!), then ultimate big-hearted forgiveness (you know I'll always love you). Again, it's the profile of an abusive husband.

Joel

Joel was one of the apocalyptic prophets. His dates are unknown, but his predictions of misery are timeless.

Warming up, he compares the travails of the final days before the Apocalypse to a plague of locusts.

> *The country is like a garden of Eden ahead of*

> them
> and a desert waste behind them.
> 2:3

Then there is the Day of Judgment. Joel's major contribution to the Bible is his contribution to the growing pile of fearful imagery about the end of time.

> *The sun will be turned into darkness,*
> *and the moon into blood,*
> *before the day of Yahweh dawns,*
> *that great and terrible day.*
> *All who call on the name of Yahweh will be saved...*
> *3:4-5*

Amos

Writing in the mid-eighth century BCE, Amos' dire prophecies were aimed at the northern tribes living in Israel. For pure spit-in-your-eye invective against sinners, he may be the best writer in the Old Testament:

> *Woe to those ensconced so snugly in Zion...*
> *Lying on their ivory beds*
> *and sprawling on their divans*
> *they dine on lambs from the flock,*
> *and stall-fattened veal;*
> *they bawl to the sound of the harp...*
> *That is why they will be the first to be exiled;*
> *the sprawlers' revelry is over.*
> *6:1-7*

"Sprawlers" is good.

Like some prior prophets, Amos repeats the warning that the Assyrians are coming. But he is such a good writer he makes it fun to hear about. Here he makes a brutal joke about the hope that Yahweh will step in at the last moment and save everyone:

> *Like a shepherd rescuing a couple of legs or a*
> *bit of an ear*
> *from the lion's mouth,*
> *so will these sons of Israel*
> *be rescued, who now loll in Samaria*
> *on the corner pillows of their divans.*
> 3:12

I like that "corner pillows" detail. It's always the best spot on the couch, the one that the selfish and self-indulgent claim.

Obadiah

Don't blink, because this book is about to go by. Written shortly after the fall of Jerusalem in 587 BCE, *Obadiah* is one of the shortest books in the Old Testament, a little over two pages. It consists of a single mouthful of threats and imprecations against the Edomites, whom Obadiah accuses of joining the Babylonians in helping to bring Jerusalem down.

Jonah[17]

One of everybody's favorites, of course. This book is probably about the prophet of the same name who was born near Nazareth in the mid-eighth century BCE. His story is a comic Passion Play. Even Yahweh seems to enjoy toying with the poor sot. It's partly because Jonah is jumpy and stupid. The perfect target for practical

---

[17] J.R.R. Tolkien was the translator of *Jonah* in The Jerusalem Bible, the translation I'm using.

jokes.

Yahweh gives him a mission: go to Ninevah (capital of Assyria) and "inform them that their wickedness has become known to me." (1:1-3) That's like telling someone to walk into a biker bar and knock over everyone's beer.

Jonah appears to know this, and decides instead to run away. That's right: Run. Away. From. Yahweh. Like, I'm *sure!* He books passage on a ship headed in the opposite direction from Ninevah. A big storm brews up, the sailors blame Jonah for causing it, and they throw him into the sea, where he is swallowed by a "great fish."

Jonah thinks he's been cast into Sheol, and launches into a prayer of fervent contrition (2:3-10), and promises he will fulfill the assignment Yahweh gave him. Then:

> *Yahweh spoke to the fish, which then vomited*
> *Jonah onto the shore.*
> 2:11

That's a punch line, if I ever heard one.

Micah

With *Micah* we again find ourselves in the time of Isaiah, about 740 BCE. Micah is a kind of rural version of Isaiah, pelting his people with visions of doom and destruction as he wanders about the countryside. He has no use for temple worship and expensive sacrifices. His rhetoric is as loud and unimaginative as a Texas radio preacher's, but he does rail equally against the primping city priesthood as well as the usual targets—Samaria, the selfish and venal rich, the pagan nations, etc.

Micah's most significant contribution to the discussion is to advocate a return to a time when the Jewish people had a more personal relationship with Yahweh. Unlike most of the other prophets, he's not talking about a return to the time of King David but a return to the time of Moses, when there were no priests, when there were no temples, and altars were where you made them. In a passage specifically rejecting the practice of making elaborate and expensive offerings, he says this:

[T]his is what Yahweh asks of you:
only this, to act justly,
to love tenderly
and to walk humbly with your God.
6:8

Nahum
Nahum is a bit of an embarrassment, because the entire book (four pages) is devoted to cheering for the wrong victory. It was written in the late 600s BCE, at a time when it seemed that Judah was on a roll. The king, Josiah, is hailed as the most devout leader since David, and he was doing well on the battlefield too. It is during his reign that the original *Book of Deuteronomy* is discovered during the course of some Temple repairs, triggering a resurgence of religious fervor in the country. Best of all, the Assyrians are getting their butts kicked by the Babylonians. Yeah! The Jews are back, man! Yahweh is on our side again!

Not. In 609 BCE, a few years after *Nahum* was written, King Josiah was killed in battle, and the Jews soon sank back into the sinful practices that caused Jeremiah to tear his hair out. Yahweh is about to lose His patience again, and soon the Babylonians will sweep in and de-populate Judah.

Habakkuk

Habakkuk succeeded Nahum as the prophet laureate of Judah. It was he who had to pick up the religious pieces after the Babylonians sacked Jerusalem the first time. None of Nahum's cock-a-doodle-dooing for him. The mood of *Habakkuk* is grim and shell-shocked. The first words of the book are "How long, Yahweh, am I to cry for help?" (1:2)

These troubles, however, prompt Habakkuk to ask a question that no one in the Bible, not even Job, has thought to ask, and I tip my hat to him for asking it: *Why evil?*

> *Why do you look on while men are treacherous,*
> *and stay silent while the evil man swallows a*
> *better man than he?*
>
> *You treat mankind like fishes in the sea,*
> *Like creeping, masterless things.*
> 1:13-14

In other words: Why does Yahweh allow evil in his Creation? Damn straight. That's the most important question of all.

Zephaniah

This mercifully short book (five and a half pages) is *the* generic sermon, the C, F, and G chords of Old Testament prophecy. Just look at the section headings for the first chapter:

- *Prelude: judgment on all creation*
- *Against the worship of alien gods*
- *Against the dignitaries of the court*
- *Against the merchants of Jerusalem*
- *Against unbelievers*

- *The day of Yahweh*
- *Conclusion: a call to conversion*

Zephaniah is a manual of style for would-be Biblical sermonizers.

Haggai

Winner of the Shortest Book of the Old Testament award (one chapter, two pages), *Haggai* was written about 520 BCE, shortly after the Babylonian exiles were allowed return to the Promised Land and the restoration of the Temple in Jerusalem. That is, for those Jews who had the strength and willingness to make the trek. To get home, they had to walk across what is today Iraq and Jordan—not a journey for weaklings. Remember too that not all the Jews in Babylon (and some were in Egypt as well) were unhappy. They'd had seventy years to make themselves comfortable, after all. How many wealthy Jews living now in Los Angeles and New York are planning sell their houses and shut down their businesses to move to Israel?

The Jews who return to Judah in Haggai's time find life hard and conditions primitive. It is demoralizing to be struggling to survive in the Promised Land! Through Haggai, Yahweh reminds them that no matter how hard their lives are their first responsibility is to rebuild the Temple in Jerusalem. Life will continue to be hard until they do this. They obey, though the resulting structure is a poor imitation of the original. Never mind, says Haggai, the main thing is that they did it. Yahweh will take it from here.

> *"I will fill this Temple with glory," says Yahweh Sabaoth...*
> *The new glory of this Temple is going to surpass the old...*
> 1:8-9

Zechariah

A contemporary of Haggai, the prophet Zechariah was a kind of Biblical science fiction writer. His book reads like a crowd of people all talking at once, rising at times to a roar of foaming ecstatic babble. There is a whole warehouse of Doctor of Divinity degrees for students willing to take on the challenge of sorting out this clamoring grab bag of symbols and allegories.

There are flying scrolls, design specifications for a perpetual lamp (you run some golden pipes from two olive branches directly into the bowl), a wicked woman hiding in a bushel, and a whole committee of talking angels.

But amidst the churning symbols and apocalyptic splutterings two really notable images pop up. One is in a short verse titled "The Messiah":

> *See now, your king comes to you;*
> *he is victorious, he is triumphant,*
> *humble and riding on a donkey...*
> 9:9

I'm guessing that a young man growing up in Bethlehem read that passage for, as we shall see, Jesus went to the trouble of procuring a donkey to ride on before his triumphant entrance into Jerusalem.

Zechariah also writes this:

> *They will look on the one whom they have*
> *pierced; they will mourn for him as for an only*
> *son...*
> 12:10

That originally came from Isaiah, but it's still eerie in its prescience because it, like *Isaiah* was written well before Jesus walked the earth. (Of course it could have been edited later, but whatever…)

As best as I can make out, the overall theme of *Zechariah* is that once the Jews have renewed their commitment to Yahweh, He will assist them in taking over the world.

Malachi
This is the last book in the Old Testament. Some scholars doubt that Malachi was a real person. His name can be construed to mean "my messenger" in Hebrew, thus making him into a kind of generic prophet. The writing seems to date from sometime after the Jews' return from their Babylonian exile, maybe as late as 420 BCE.

In any case, the book is a short but harsh rebuke from Yahweh directed at lazy, greedy priests. Apparently, there is a problem with the quality of offerings being presented to the altar by some priests. They're supposed to slaughter the finest animals for this ceremony, but some think they can offer blind or lame or diseased animals and (presumably) keep the best for themselves. Yahweh threatens to defrock them if they don't start behaving.

Also there is a problem with some lay people coming up short with their tithes. Be miserly with Me and I will be miserly to you, warns Yahweh.

Finally, Yahweh reminds everyone that they only have a limited time. Speaking as Yahweh Saboath, the name He uses when He's angry, He warns that The Day of Judgment is coming:

> *For the day is coming now, burning like a*
> *furnace; and all the arrogant and the evildoers*

will be like stubble. The day that is coming is going to burn them up, says Yahweh Sabaoth, leaving them neither root nor stalk. But for you who fear my name, the sun of righteousness will shine out with healing in its rays; you will leap like calves going out to pasture. You will trample on the wicked, who will be like ashes under feet on the day I am preparing, says Yahweh Sabaoth.

3:19-21

With *Malachi,* the Old Testament comes to an end, leaving an undeniable impression of exhaustion, as if in the telling of the rise and fall of the Jews, the authors and editors are as spiritually depleted as the people whose story they have told.

The New Testament

Introduction

The New Testament begins about 500 years after the Old Testament ends. It covers a period of about sixty years, compared with the Old Testament's span of some 1400 years.

It's hardly surprising, then, that the New Testament lacks the historical sweep and drama of the Old. The major events of the New Testament are the Crucifixion and the Resurrection, which, while stunning and earth-shaking, can't compete with Creation, Exodus and the tempestuous relationship between Yahweh and his intransigent people; with the rise of King David and the fall of Jerusalem.

While the Old Testament has the feel of a tattered family album, the New Testament reads more like a textbook. It's a focused and well-organized collection of stories and sermons bent on convincing the reader of the divinity of Jesus Christ and the necessity of following his teachings if you expect to have any chance at all of a decent after-life. It's also much less fun to read than the Old Testament.

It has its moments, of course. The week of the Passion, which recounts the events triggered by Jesus' decision to come into Jerusalem and face his enemies, is the core of the story and compelling reading. During that week Jesus confronts his enemies, is betrayed by one of his disciples, is arrested by the Jewish authorities and subjected to humiliation, defeat, death and ignominy. His ultimate victory, the Resurrection, is probably the greatest surprise ending in all of history.

The part of the New Testament actually devoted to recounting

Jesus' life is fairly short. It consists of the Four Gospels, supposedly eye-witness accounts of Jesus' wanderings in the hinterlands of Judah and his final showdown with the Pharisees in Jerusalem. The Gospel narratives overlap each other and show signs of major touching-up. Scholars think that the writing of them didn't begin until decades after Jesus' departure from the scene and there's no knowing to what degree they are based on Mark, Matthew, Luke and Johns' actual eye witness accounts.

As we will see later on, none of this would have mattered very much without Paul, a man who never met Jesus face-to-face. First, however, we're going to look at the Gospels. The first three—*Matthew, Mark,* and *Luke*—are called the Synoptic Gospels because they tell more or less the same story. The fourth gospel, *John*, is unique unto itself, and may have come from another Christian tradition altogether. We'll talk about that when we get there.

Though most Bibles put *Matthew* first, we're going to start with *Mark*, because it's the oldest.

The Gospel According to Saint Mark

Mark is by far the shortest of the Gospels, mainly because Mark's focus is on the end of the story—the last week of Jesus' life during which he is arrested, tried, crucified, and resurrected. In his haste to get to this part of the story Mark skips over some of the best parts of the other gospel narratives. The virgin birth? For Mark it never happened. The manger, the three wise men, the star of Bethlehem? Forget about it. All Mark cares about is what happened to Jesus when he traveled to Jerusalem.

Mark is also not interested in being dramatic. In relating the two years of Jesus' wandering about in northern Judah, Mark flips through the various parables and miracles as if they were so many 3x5 cards. It almost reads like a police report. Mark doesn't care about using rhetoric or embellishments to get his readers worked up. For him, the facts of who Jesus was, what he said, and what he did are all that are required to make you want to be a Christian.

The first ten chapters of *Mark* consist of a brief description of Jesus' adventures as he wends his way through the countryside, creating a groundswell of excitement that perhaps he really is the long-awaited Christ or Messiah.[18] This section of *Mark* is full of thumbnail descriptions of the various miracles Jesus performed in northern Judah during his sojourn in the countryside. Also included are some of his parables—simple, often homely little stories that illustrate a point about man's relationship to God.

---

[18] The long-awaited savior of the Jews. Often imagined as the second coming of King David.

The Gerasene Demoniac

One of my favorite miracles (found in 5:1-20) is called "The Gerasene demoniac." It goes like this: In the country of the Gerasenes lived a man possessed by many demons. He lived in the tombs, howling and gashing himself with stones. The people tried to chain him up but he snapped the chains and ran back to the tombs. When the demoniac saw Jesus approaching, he ran up to him. The demons, afraid, spoke out of the man's mouth, begging not to be sent away. But they saw that Jesus intended to cast them out no matter what. It happened that there was a herd of about two thousand pigs feeding nearby. The demons begged Jesus to send them into the pigs, and he granted their wish. The terrified pigs "charged down the cliff into the lake, and there they were drowned." (5:13) The suddenly cured demoniac sat on the ground, a whole man again. The swineherds were impressed but on the whole not pleased. They implored Jesus to leave the neighborhood, and he got into his boat with the disciples and sailed away. End of story. Moral: Even doing good can have unintended consequences.

Sometimes Jesus and his friends seem to be the main benefactors of a miracle. Here is what he did for Simon's mother-in-law:

> *On leaving the synagogue, he went with James and John straight to the house of Simon and Andrew. Now Simon's mother-in-law had gone to bed with fever, and they told him about her straightaway. He went to her, took her by the hand and helped her up. And the fever left her and she began to wait on them.*
> 1:29-31

'Feeling better, hon? Swell. Now how about some wine and

cheese.'

The Bleeding Woman
Sometimes a miracle can have the dramatic force of a well-told story:

> One day a synagogue official named Jairus approaches Jesus. His daughter is dying and he begs Jesus to save her life. Jesus agrees, and they set out for Jairus' house. By now Jesus has achieved some renown, and crowds follow him wherever he goes. In the crowd is a woman who has been bleeding for twelve years (the source of the bleeding is not specified, but surely it's some sort of menstrual problem) and has been trying, without success, to get close to Jesus. 'If I could just touch his clothes,' she thinks. She darts forward and touches Jesus' cloak. Instantly the bleeding stops. "Immediately aware that power had gone out from him, Jesus turned around in the crowd and said, 'Who touched my clothes?'" (5:30-31) That seems like a silly question to the disciples, who point out that he's being jostled constantly by the crowd. But Jesus knows better, and insists on finding out who touched him. The woman finally comes forward, terrified that she's going to be punished somehow. Instead, Jesus bids her to go in peace, free from her complaint.
>
> Now all this time Jairus must have been going out of his mind. His daughter is *dying,* and here Jesus is wasting time chatting it up with the crowd. Sure enough, some people come from Jairus' house.

They report that the girl has died. 'Tell Jesus not to bother coming. Save him a trip.' they mutter. But Jesus insists on coming anyway. Here the narrative handles the drama most skillfully. The scene at Jairus' house is chaotic, everyone is weeping and wailing. The perfect time for a thunderbolt of a miracle, wouldn't you think? But no. Instead, Jesus merely says, "Why all this commotion and crying? The child is not dead, but asleep." And he goes into her bedroom and brings her out by the hand.

Sometimes the quiet miracles are the best.

Parables

Then there are the parables. Many of them are like riddles that listeners have to ponder to reveal the meaning. Here is an example, called "Parable of the lamp":

> *"Would you bring in a lamp to put it under a tub or under the bed? Surely you will put it on the lampstand? For there is nothing hidden but it must be disclosed, nothing kept secret except to be brought to light. If anyone has ears to hear, let him listen to this."*

4:21-23

Give up? Answer: Jesus is the lamp. You wouldn't use a lamp to heat water or warm a bed. You use it to dispel darkness. Why would he be brought into the world except to illuminate the truth?

Here's another, called "Parable of the seed growing by itself":

> *"This is what the kingdom of God is like. A*

> *man throws seed on the land. Night and day, while he sleeps, when he is awake, the seed is sprouting and growing; how, he does not know. Of its own accord the land produces first the shoot, then the ear, then the full grain in the ear. And when the crop is ready, he loses no time: he starts to reap because the harvest has come."*

4:26-29

When a farmer sows seed, he has nothing but faith to assure him that it will become a crop. There's no need to understand the process. Likewise, to enter the kingdom of God it is necessary only to have faith.

That's a sweet idea about God's relationship to man and vice-versa, but it only takes a couple of crop failures to make that farmer think about pitching a few prayers in Baal's direction, just to increase his chances.

For the really tough parables, Jesus sometimes provides the answer.

> *"Listen to me, all of you, and understand. Nothing that goes into a man from outside can make him unclean; it is the things that come out of a man that make him unclean. If anyone has ears to hear, let him listen to this.*

7:14-16

'Huh?' is the disciples' collective response. So Jesus lays it out. Things that come into a man from the outside cannot make him unclean because they come in through his mouth, go into his stomach, and he shits them out. Conversely, it is the things that come *out* of a man—"fornication, theft, murder, adultery, avarice, malice, deceit, indecency, envy, slander, pride, folly" (7:22-23)—that make him unclean.

Notice that this parable and the one about the bleeding woman pretty much unwrite much of *Leviticus,* that testament to the fear and loathing of prohibited foods and menstruating women.

Let's move on to the last week of Jesus' life—the Passion—which for Mark is by far the most important part of the story. The drama starts with Jesus' entrance into Jerusalem.

Turning the Tables
Once he passes through the gates, Jesus doesn't waste any time. He does what is probably the most provocative thing he could have done: he goes straight to the Temple. Over the years a marketplace had grown up there, which Jesus thinks is an affront to the solemn, sacred purpose of the Temple. He strides into the market,

> *...and began driving out those who were selling and buying there; he upset the tables of the money changers and the chairs of those who were selling pigeons. Nor would he allow anyone to carry anything through the Temple.*

11:15-17

Now of course the chief priests have known for days that Jesus and his horde are on the way to Jerusalem. They have little choice but to wait and see what happens. In trashing the Temple market Jesus makes their worst fears come true: He really is out to overturn the established order. They begin to discuss how best to do away with him (11:18).

So the stage is set. Jesus has come to Jerusalem to die—he's already told his disciples this three times, in 8:31-33, 9:30-32, and 10:32-34—and in dying, bring the corrupt Jewish establishment down with him. He is a suicide bomber, just with no bombs. In a sense, the priests and Jesus are in complete agreement: he wants to die and they want to kill him.

This is a game being played with loaded dice. We've seen this before, in *Genesis*, when Yahweh would not allow Pharaoh to accede to Moses' demand that he let the Israelites go. Every time Pharaoh seemed to waver, Yahweh "hardened his heart" and made him refuse to release them. Something similar is going on here. Jesus is not going to give the Pharisees and the Sadducees (the two principal priestly brotherhoods) the chance to listen to his ministry and make up their own minds about whether or not he is the Messiah. No, he is going to provoke them by defying their laws, humiliating them in public debate, and challenging their authority by declaring that their interpretation of Torah law is no longer relevant. He leaves them no choice but to lay plans for his destruction.

Still, it's fun to watch it play out. The debates between the priests and Jesus at the Temple are well-staged. The Pharisees are trying to trap Jesus into saying something blasphemous or treasonous so they can arrest him. The drill is they ask him a difficult question, he refutes it, and they, fuming with frustration, withdraw into a huddle to compose another question. Jesus has an agile mind and is not above toying with them as he cuts them to pieces. My favorite is the oft-quoted "render unto Caesar" exchange. Here's the question:

> "Tell us your opinion, then. Is it permissible to pay taxes to Caesar or not?"

22:17-18

They think they've got him ensnared. This is one of those 'Have you stopped beating your wife?' type questions, to which there is no correct 'yes' or 'no' answer. Here's how he responds:

> *"Let me see the money you pay the tax with."*
> *They handed him a denarius, and he said,*
> *"Whose head is this? Whose name?"*
> *"Caesar's," they replied. "Very well, give*
> *back to Caesar what belongs to Caesar—and to*
> *God what belongs to God."*

22:17-21

'If it's got Caesar's picture on it, it must be his. Give it back to him.' Very smooth.

Eventually the priests withdraw and leave Jesus alone with the crowd that has gathered. Only then does he utter the blasphemy the priests have been trying to pry from him. It is a sacred tenet of the Jewish faith that the Messiah, or Christ, be descended from King David. Here Jesus dismisses it in a few words:

> *Later, while teaching in the Temple, Jesus said,*
> *"How can the scribes maintain that the Christ*
> *is the son of David? David himself, moved by*
> *the Holy Spirit, said:*
>
>> *The Lord said to my Lord:*
>> *Sit at my right hand*
>> *and I will put your enemies*
>> *under your feet.*
>
> *David calls him Lord, in what way then can he*

> *be his son?"*
12:35-37

That's a little tortured, I know. But if you pick at it a little the meaning slides out. The verse Jesus' is quoting is from *Psalms* 110:1. In this verse, the first "Lord" is God and the second "Lord" is the Christ. This shows that Christ cannot possibly be David's son because David addresses him as Lord.

Is it clearer now? No? Let's move on.

Good News and Bad News
The word "gospel" comes from the Old English "godspell," meaning good news or glad tidings, something that evangelical Christians like to emphasize. But the very fact Jesus Christ has appeared signifies also that life on earth is about to come to an end. For some—for many—this will come as bad news.

One of Jesus' jobs is to issue the warning. The playfulness that he showed in toying with the priests at the Temple is gone. His mood is dark, and the language stark and chilling. When the Apocalypse begins, he says:

> *"...if a man is on the housetop, he must not come down to go into the house to collect any of his belongings; if a man is in the fields, he must not turn back to fetch his cloak. Alas for those with child, or with babies at the breast, when those days come! Pray that this may not be in winter. For in those days there will be such distress as, until now, has not been equaled since the beginning when God created the world, nor ever will be again."*

13:14-20

Oops

Here whoever is managing the narrative makes a huge tactical mistake. He allows Jesus to issue a testable prediction. He is talking about all the stuff that's going to happen as the End nears ("…the sun will darken, the moon will lose its brightness…" etc.) Then he says:

> *"I tell you solemnly, before this generation has passed away all these things will have taken place."*

13:30

That lays out a time line of thirty years or so, max. Hearing this, his disciples would be justified in expecting that in their own lifetimes they would witness the destruction of the world, the casting down to hell of the sinners, the redemption of the faithful, and the beginning of eternal life in heaven. But…two thousand years later we're still waiting. Later on you'll see how much trouble this discrepancy causes Paul as he goes about the work of assembling Christianity.

While the reigning priests of Jerusalem are busy planning Jesus' demise, Jesus has been staying at the house of Simon in Bethany (Lazarus lives there as well). At dinner one day Jesus is in a relatively light-hearted mood. A woman approaches with "an alabaster jar of very costly ointment, pure nard," (14:5) and pours it on his head, a gesture of love and respect. Some of the men at the table are appalled. Nard (the aromatic extract of a flowering plant called spikenard, found in the Himalayas) is costly stuff, and here she is wasting a whole jar of it on Jesus. Somebody makes the comment that the jar should have been sold and the money given to the poor.

Jesus' reply is interesting:

> *You have the poor with you always, and you can be kind to them whenever you wish, but you will not always have me.*

14:7-8

Go ahead, spoil me a little, you won't have me for long.

The Last Supper
Everybody knows this story, but just in case you're from Mars.... In the days leading up to Passover, Jesus arranges to have supper with his disciples. While they're eating, he informs them that one of them is going to betray him. While they try to process this shocking news, Jesus performs the first celebration of the Eucharist. He blesses a loaf of bread, breaks it, and offers it to the disciples, saying, "Take it. This is my body." Then he takes a cup of wine, blesses it, and offers it to them. "This is my blood, the blood of the covenant, which is to be poured out for many." (14:22-25)

The reenactment of this moment is the most sacred rite in all Christendom. Roman Catholics call it Communion and are taught that the wafers and wine they are offered at each Mass are *literally* the flesh and blood of Jesus, having been transubstantiated in the course of the rite. Other Christian faiths celebrate the Eucharist but regard the bread and the wine as merely symbolic of the flesh and blood of Jesus.

The dire drum roll of Passion Week intensifies. Taking Peter, James, and John, Jesus goes to the garden of Gethsemane and prays to God to "Take this cup away from me," (14:36), i.e. don't make me go through the agony of the crucifixion. The narrative does not give us God's response, but obviously the answer was 'no.'

After his conference with God, Jesus returns to where the disciples are (shamefully) sleeping. While he is standing there, remonstrating Peter, a motley gang of men, led by the treacherous disciple Judas, approaches. Judas points Jesus out and the men arrest him.

Jesus is taken before the Sanhedrin (an assembly of priests with official powers) and interrogated. Under questioning, he admits (for the first time in the gospel narrative!) that he is the Christ.

> *"Are you the Christ,"* he [the high priest] *said, "the Son of the Blessed One?" "I am," said Jesus," and you will see the Son of Man seated at the right hand of the Power and coming with the clouds of heaven."*

14:61-62

The priests howl with outrage and rush at Jesus and begin beating him.

The next day they take him before the Roman authority, Pontius Pilate, and demand that he punish Jesus for the treasonous claim that he is the king of the Jews. Jesus doesn't deny it.

The Crucifixion
Pilate, feeling he has no choice, sentences Jesus to crucifixion. Immediately he is led to a place called Golgotha (traditionally thought of as a small hill, but Mark doesn't mention that). Also, in *Mark*, Jesus doesn't carry his own cross. A passer-by named Simon of Cyrene is enlisted to do it for him.

The Roman guards nail him to the cross, and his agony begins. Three hours into his torment he lifts his head and cries out, "My God, my God, why have you deserted me?" (15:34) Piteous as this sounds, it's also an unbelievably clever thing to say because this is a direct quote from *Psalm 22:1*, wherein David, in a moment of imagined agony, cries out in pained bewilderment to Yahweh. In quoting David, Jesus emphasizes his claim to be the Messiah, the next coming of a King David-like monarch.

The Resurrection
Mark's account of what happens next is straightforward and brief, but that does not lessen its significance or power. The Resurrection is *the* central event on which Christianity hangs its hat (or mitre).

Everybody knows the basics of this event, but just in case: Jesus was crucified on Friday. On the morning of following Monday three women—Mary Magdalene, Mary the mother of James, and Salome[19]—go to Jesus' tomb to anoint him. To their surprise, they see that the stone sealing the tomb had been rolled away.

> *On entering the tomb they saw a young man in a white robe seated on the right-hand side, and they were struck with amazement. But he said to them, "There is no need for alarm. You are looking for Jesus of Nazareth, who was crucified; he has risen, he is not here. See, here is the place where they laid him. But you*

---

[19] It's hard to pin down who Salome was. There were two disciples named James, and the afore-mentioned Mary is obviously the mother of one of them. A man named Zebedee is mentioned as the father of the other James. Salome appears to be the wife of Zebedee, making her the mother of the second James.

> *must go and tell his disciples and Peter. He is going before you to Galilee; it is there you will see him, just as he told you."*

16:5-8

The three women run away, "frightened out of their wits," too frightened to say anything to anyone. But presently Jesus reveals himself to Mary Magdalene, and soon after to the eleven remaining Apostles (Judas having removed himself).

Without the startling claim that Jesus arose from the dead three days after his crucifixion, the Christian religion is just a cultish scuffle among rabbis about what is allowed under Torah law and what is not.

Snakes Alive!
Mark ends with a strange coda, thought by scholars to have been appended much later than the original text. Here it is:

> *"These are the signs that will be associated with believers: in my name they will cast out devils; they will have the gift of tongues; they will pick up snakes in their hands, and be unharmed should they drink deadly poison; they will lay their hands on the sick, who will recover."*

16:17-18

This passage may have been added later, but to many Christians it *must* be true because it's in the Bible. We wouldn't have Appalachian Pentecostalism and mid-western tent revivals without it.

The Gospel According to Saint Matthew

Compared to the spare style of *Mark, Matthew* is "JESUS, The Movie." Matthew relishes in giving Jesus the full Lives of the Saints workup. The narrative unfolds as if fulfilling the requirements of a formula for the life of a Messiah. A hagiography of Jesus should begin with a genealogy showing him to be a direct descendent of Abraham and David. (Again, Jesus insists that proving that he is descended from David isn't necessary, but Matthew goes ahead and does it anyway.) His birth should be miraculous event, attended by great signs and portents, such as the star that leads the wise men from the East to Bethlehem. He should be betrayed, persecuted, and martyred. His life, in every respect, should be shown to be fulfilling the numerous Old Testament prophecies about the Messiah.

Unlike *Mark, Matthew* includes an account of Jesus' birth by a virgin. Matthew gets very solemn and awestruck about this because it appears to fulfill a prophecy in *Isaiah 7:14* ("…the maiden is with child and will soon give birth to a son whom she will call Immanuel"). For Matthew, "Immanual" is another name for the Messiah, and since he believes Jesus is the Messiah, Immanual is another name for Jesus.

(A microbiology problem that Matthew doesn't seem to have considered is that if Jesus was born of a virgin he couldn't possibly be descended from David. But let's not quibble. Some of the greatest stories have little paradoxes like this.)

When Mary tells Joseph she is pregnant yet is still a virgin, he is understandably skeptical. There were three courses of action open to him. One, he could demand that she prove her claim to be a virgin, as provided for in *Deuteronomy* 22:13-21. If she is found to be lying, the penalty is death by stoning. Two, he could formally divorce her by going before the magistrate and accusing her of adultery. Again, death by stoning. Thirdly, he could simply tell her to go away, keeping the whole matter as quiet as possible. Not surprisingly he chooses number three:

> *...being a man of honor and wanting to spare her publicity, he decided to divorce her informally.*

1:19-20

Later an angel comes to Joseph and convinces him that Mary is not lying, so he takes her back. Eventually, Mary gives birth to four other boys, so obviously the marriage recovered from its shaky start.

Who is This Man?
As Matthew portrays him, Jesus outshines Moses and David as the most interesting character in the Bible. He is a complex, contradictory man; a mini-Yahweh, in some ways. He has that quality of rapidly reversing polarities that Yahweh has: sweet/angry, reasonable/irrational, accessible/unapproachable, the kind teacher/the scathing master—contradictions that in the right combinations can accumulate into electrifying charisma.

He's repeatedly hailed by his disciples as the Messiah, the next coming of a King David-like leader who will restore the Jews to their rightful status as the Chosen People, the highest form of humanity, the most beloved of God's creations. Jesus himself cleverly sidesteps the question of whether he is or is not the Messiah, basically telling people to judge him by his character and acts. He repeatedly refers to himself as "the son of man," a term used many times in the Old Testament, and so ambiguous that it causes theologians to foam at the mouth.

Pagans Need Not Apply

Part of Jesus' mission is to prepare his disciples for their future ministry. In instructing them he sometimes shows a distaste for non-Jews that you'd hardly expect from the savior of the world. Here he is giving instructions to his disciples as they prepare to go out and spread the word that the Day of Judgment is almost here:

> *"Do not turn your steps to pagan territory, and do not enter any Samaritan town; go rather to the lost sheep of the House of Israel."*
> 10:5-6

His dislike for non-Jews flares up again as he attempts to avoid a Canaanite woman seeking his help:

> *Then out came a Canaanite woman...and started shouting, "Sir, Son of David, take pity on me. My daughter is tormented by a devil." But he answered her not a word. And his disciples went and pleaded with him. "Give her what she wants," they said, "because she is shouting after us." He said in reply, "I was sent only to the lost sheep of the House of Israel." But the woman had come up and was kneeling at his feet. "Lord," she said, "help me." He replied, "It is not fair to take the children's food* [the word of God] *and throw it to the house dogs."* [i.e. pagans] *She retorted, "Ah yes, sir; but even house dogs can eat the scraps that fall from their master's table."*

> *Then Jesus answered her, "Woman, you have great faith. Let your wish be granted." And from that moment her daughter was well again.*

15:21-28

In the end he threw this clever dog a scrap, but his contempt for the pagans is unchanged.

Sermon on the Mount

More important than the miracles are Jesus' teachings. His most famous sermon, The Sermon on the Mount (Chapters 5-7), is the single most glorious utterance in the New Testament. It is wise, good-humored, direct, and persuasive. Listening to it, or reading it, you find yourself wanting to follow this man. This is how a spiritual leader is supposed to sound!

The theme of the sermon is the examination and re-interpretation of the original Commandments and other fundamental Jewish laws. The laws are still valid, Jesus says, but they must be observed within the heart as well as for public display. The law against adultery, for example, ought to be expanded to include adulterous thoughts. Listen to what he has to say about oaths:

> *Again, you have learned how it was said to our ancestors: You must not break your oath, but must fulfill your oaths to the Lord. But I say this to you: do not swear at all, either by heaven, since that is God's throne; or by the earth, since that is his footstool; or by Jerusalem, since that is the city of the great king. Do not swear by your own head either, since you cannot turn a single hair white or black. All you need say is 'Yes' if you mean yes,*

> *'No' if you mean no; anything more than this comes from the evil one.*
> 5:33-37

People in the Bible don't usually speak with such disarming calm and directness.

But the best part of the Sermon on the Mount is the part about the birds and the flowers. This is simply a gust of generosity, good sense and compassion that is still nearly as irresistible now as it must have been when it was first spoken in Galilee. Listen:

> *"That is why I am telling you not to worry about your life and what you are to eat, nor about your body and how you are to clothe it. Surely life means more than food, and the body more than clothing! Look at the birds in the sky. They do not sow or reap or gather into barns; yet your heavenly Father feeds them. Are you not worth much more than they are? Can any of you, for all his worrying, add one single cubit to his span of life? And why worry about clothing? Think of the flowers growing in the fields; they never have to work or spin; yet I assure you that not even Solomon in all his regalia was robed like one of these. Now if that is how God clothes the grass in the field which is there today and thrown into the furnace tomorrow, will he not much more look after you, you men of little faith?... So do not worry about tomorrow: tomorrow will take care of itself. Each day has enough trouble of its own."*

6:24-34

It must have been amazing for people used to the strictures of orthodox Jewish teaching to hear Jesus say these things. Yet this famous sermon may be more seductive than substantive. If you advise homeless people, for example, "not to worry about your life and what you are to eat, nor about your body and how you are to clothe it," they may not take it very kindly.

The Lord's Prayer
The Sermon on the Mount is also where the Lord's Prayer is introduced. For most people the Lord's Prayer is a rote recitation like the Pledge of Allegiance. Yet it contains some interesting metaphysical information as well as a deft modification of Yahweh's public image.

The Lord's Prayer uses the word "Father" for God. But another name for Him is Yahweh, the spiteful god who once killed seventy villagers because they hesitated to rejoice on the return of the Ark from the Philistines (*I Samuel* 6:19). The name Father is a subtle re-branding. A father can be expected to express love from time to time.

And yet there are still some bruises left over from the suffering that this "Father" inflicted on the Jews in the Old Testament. At the end of the Lord's Prayer[20] it says, "And do not put us to the test/

---

[20] **The Lord's Prayer**
"Our Father in heaven,
May your name be held holy,
Your kingdom come,
Your will be done,
On earth as in heaven.
Give us today our daily bread.

but save us from the evil one." (6:13) (The King James Translation says: "And lead us not into temptation, but deliver us from evil.") There's a long history behind that meek request. So many times in the Old Testament Yahweh tempts or lets or makes His people do the wrong thing and then punishes them for it, to show them that He is in charge. What else is the forbidden fruit in the Garden of Eden but a temptation? When we recite the Lord's Prayer we are pleading with God not to do that anymore.

"I Bring a Sword"

The infatuation we feel after hearing the Sermon on the Mount begins to fade a bit as Jesus' gets into his Judgment Day teachings. Far from being the Messiah whose message is love and whose mission is to rescue, this is the Jesus who says:

> *Do not suppose that I have come to bring peace to the earth: it is not peace I have come to bring, but a sword. For I have come to set a man against his father, a daughter against her mother, a daughter-in-law against her mother-in-law. A man's enemies will be those of his own household.*
> 10:34-36

Jesus is the agent of heaven responsible for the business of harvesting those few (Jewish) souls who are willing, by an act of faith, to give themselves over to him. Those who are not saved, he says bluntly, will be thrown away.

And forgive us our debts,
As we have forgiven those who are in debt to us.
And do not put us to the test,
But save us from the evil one."

> *"Again, the kingdom of heaven is like a dragnet cast into the sea that brings in a haul of all kinds. When it is full, the fishermen haul it ashore; then, sitting down, they collect the good ones in a basket and throw away those that are no use. This is how it will be at the end of time: the angels will appear and separate the wicked from the just to throw them into the blazing furnace where there will be weeping and grinding of teeth."*
> 13:47-50

It appears that the experiment with humanity will soon be over. It got off to a bad start with Adam and Eve and never recovered. Over and over humankind has proved itself to be perverse and unreliable. God is getting ready to trash the whole project, and Jesus has been sent to save who he can.

How's Hell Coming Along?

Just fine, thank you very much. We got a peek at it in the passage quoted above. We've been trying to keep track of its development, and by the time of the gospels it's a finished product, ready to receive deserving customers.

You'll remember that the idea is rooted in an actual place, the Valley of Ben-Hinnom, which we first ran into in *II Kings 23*, a horrible place where at times human sacrifices were performed and dead bodies were thrown to be burned. The Hebrew name Hinnom, when translated into Greek, is Gehenna. Gehenna when translated into English is Hell. And the gospels are rich with references to Hell. Jesus uses the word eleven times. The most hair-raising instance is in *Mark 9:48,* where, drawing upon the image of worms that feed forever on the bodies of the damned, first used in *Isaiah 66:24*, he says:

> *And if your eye should cause you to sin, tear it out; it is better for you to enter into the kingdom of God with one eye, than to have two eyes and be thrown into hell, where "their worm does not die nor fire go out."*

Passion Week

Matthew's rendition of the Passion is faithful to Mark's, but adds a few flourishes. For example, as Jesus prepares to enter he calls for someone to find a donkey for him. Why? Because of the prophecy in *Zechariah 9:9*:

> *See now, your king comes to you;*
> *he is victorious, he is triumphant,*
> *humble and riding on a donkey.*

It was a master stroke. The Old Testament says that the Messiah is supposed to enter Jerusalem on a donkey. Now here comes Jesus, a man whom many call the Messiah. And look, he's riding a donkey! So it must be true! "Great crowds of people spread their cloaks on the road, while others were cutting branches from the trees and spreading them in his path." (21:8-9) Passion Week is off to a good start.

Matthew also cites *Isaiah* to bolster the case for Jesus as the Messiah. Here's the crucial passage:

> *And yet ours were the sufferings he bore,*
> *Ours the sorrows he carried.*
> *But we, we thought of him as someone punished,*

> *Struck by God, and brought low.*
> *Yet he was pierced through for our faults,*
> *Crushed for our sins.*
> *On him lies a punishment that brings us peace,*
> *And through his wounds we are healed...*

Isaiah 53:4-5

"Pierced" is particularly eerie, given that *Isaiah* was written (or compiled) in about 700 BCE.

What Happens Next?

We've previously discussed the problems with Jesus' prophecies. In *Matthew* these problems are even more apparent. Jesus says several times that the decisive events signifying the end of the world will take place soon:

> *"I tell you solemnly, you will not have gone the round of the towns of Israel before the Son of Man comes."*
> 10:23

Later, he tells them:

> *"I tell you solemnly, there are some of these standing here who will not taste death before they see the Son of Man coming with his kingdom."*
> 16:28

And finally:

> *I tell you solemnly, before this generation has passed away all these things will have taken place.*

24:34-35

There seems to be no question that he believed that the Day of Judgment would fall within the mortal life span of at least some of his disciples. They certainly believed it. Yet they would all be dead before the gospels were set to paper. But there the prophecy sits.

That epithet, by the way—"Son of Man—" is a name Jesus uses often, usually in a context where he is referring to himself. It's deliberately ambiguous, even coy. If he comes straight out and calls himself the Christ or Messiah, he probably would be charged with blasphemy by the Pharisees, who are waiting for him to commit such a crime. Yet he needs to call himself *something*. "Son of man" occurs 114 times in the Old Testament, and by the time we get to the New Testament it has taken on the nimbus of a sacred name. Most importantly, it is a safe name. Not until the trial that leads to his crucifixion does he call himself the Messiah.

It's handy that the Bible itself provides us with a simple test for prophets (*Deuteronomy* 18:21-22), which Jesus himself invoked during the Sermon on the Mount: You'll know you were listening to a false prophet if what he says does not come true.

The Gospel According to Saint Luke

The Gospel According to Saint Luke doesn't add much to our understanding of Jesus' story. As with *Matthew*, *Luke* wholly lifts large portions of *Mark's* text. In fact, about 50% of *Luke* is copied out of *Mark*. But Luke wasn't interested in being original. He was interested in shaping the story for a particular audience: the Roman authorities, specifically an official named Theophilus.

In the Prologue Luke explains to Theophilus that by now there are many versions of Jesus' life and acts, and that he, Luke, has gone over them all and is prepared to "write a more ordered account...so that your Excellency may learn how well-founded the teaching is that you have received." (1:1-4)

Presumably because a Roman official wouldn't be interested in Jewish history, *Luke* does not emphasize Jesus' fulfillment of Old Testament Jewish prophecies. Luke was more interested in portraying Jesus as an extraordinary supernatural manifestation. In effect, he is saying to Theophilus: 'Look here, our Deity has sent us a message; this man, Jesus of Nazareth, is the agent; we must look into what he says.'

After the Prologue, *Luke* gives us a hagiography of Jesus' life much like Matthew's. However, there are a few differences. For example, *Luke* is the only gospel that gives us a glimpse of Jesus as a boy. On a trip to Jerusalem, the twelve-year-old Jesus sneaks away from his parents and goes to the Temple to engage in dialogue with the wise men there. "...and all who heard him were astounded at his intelligence and his replies." (2:47-48) A twelve-year-old know-it-all: what's so surprising about that?

Luke's rendition of the Passion (Jesus' arrest, trial, and crucifixion) is by far the best of the gospels. Luke had a cinematic eye for the right detail. For example, *Mark* and *Matthew* both describe a brief struggle at the moment of Jesus' arrest. In the confusion one of his followers lashes out with a sword and cuts off the ear of one thug in the arresting mob. Only in *Luke*, however, does Jesus reach out to touch and heal the man's wound. (22:51)

Luke even gives us an imagined look into how Jesus' jailers were treating him:

> *Meanwhile the men who guarded Jesus were mocking and beating him. They blindfolded him and questioned him. "Play the prophet," they said. "Who hit you then?" And they continued heaping insults on him.*

22:63-64

Also in *Luke* we find Hell in its finished form as a place of tormenting flames. Here Jesus is telling a parable about the rich man in the afterlife. Note that the ancient word Sheol has been replaced by the Greek term Hades, probably because Theophilus, who is Luke's intended audience, would have been familiar with it:

> *"In his torment in Hades*[21] *he looked up and saw Abraham a long way off with Lazarus in his bosom. So he cried out, 'Father Abraham, pity me and send Lazarus to dip the tip of his*

---

[21] Notice that Luke uses the Greek word "Hades" instead of the traditional Jewish word "Sheol," to denote the place of the dead, probably because Theophilus, the Roman official to whom this account is addressed, would have been more familiar with it.

> *finger in water and cool my tongue, for I am in agony in these flames."*

16:23-25

History does not record what kindness, if any, Theophilus showed the Jews as a result of Luke's skillful presentation.

By the way, when Luke finished his gospel, he wasn't done contributing to the Bible. Most commentators credit *Acts of the Apostles* to him as well. We'll get to that later.

The Gospel According to Saint John

> *In the beginning was the Word:*
> *the Word was with God*
> *and the Word was God.*

1:1

> *The Word was made flesh,*
> *he lived among us, and we saw his glory,*
> *the glory that is his as the only Son of the*
> *Father,*
> *full of grace and truth.*

1:14

We're not in Kansas anymore.

The gospels of *Matthew, Mark*, and *Luke* (known as the Synoptic Gospels) were written by Jews trying to convince other Jews that Jesus was the Messiah.

The Gospel According to Saint John was written by a man (or men) who believed that Jesus was an aspect of God in human form. That's a big difference.

John is the gospel of Christian mystics. *John* is the gospel of Christian fundamentalists. *John* is the gospel of the placards at sporting events. *John* is the Bible on peyote.

Introducing...the Trinity!
Scholars think that *John* was written late in the first or mid-second century C.E. By this later date the idea of who Jesus was had fermented beyond the assertion that he was the Jewish Messiah. Now he's not only the Messiah, but he is God incarnate, part of a

trinity which includes God the Father, Jesus the Son, and the Advocate or Holy Spirit. In other words, by the time *John* was written, Christianity was a religion.

The concepts of God as the Father, and Jesus as the Son were broadly hinted at in the Synoptic Gospels. But in *John* these ideas burn white-hot; they are part of the assemblage of the Godhead, and in 14:26 the third member is announced:

> *I have said these things to you*
> *while still with you;*
> *but the Advocate, the Holy Spirit,*
> *whom the Father will send in my name*
> *will teach you everything*
> *and remind you of all I have said to you*

14:25-26

A Whole Different Kind of Gospel
Reading *John*, it doesn't take long to figure out why it's set aside from the Synoptic Gospels, *Matthew, Mark*, and *Luke. John* only loosely refers to the narrative that the three others vie to tell best. It sets itself apart right from the opening, "In the beginning was the Word…." This is no less than a re-telling of the Creation story, though completely devoid of images or myth. It goes back to a moment in eternity before there was a Trinity, when the creative force was a duality called Word/God (this dual partnership is also invoked in *Proverbs,* Chapter 8) in which God is the pure creative force and the Word its manifest articulation. This is Creation as Plato might have imagined it, a weightless transaction between abstract absolutes.

John skips over the messy business of biography—Mary claiming to be a virgin, Joseph's gentle skepticism about that, the heartrending plight of a homeless couple forced to have their baby in a feeding trough—and starts the story of Jesus' career with him already wandering around collecting disciples.

There are plenty of other differences between *John* and the three previous Gospels. For example, in the Last Supper scene of *John* there is no offering of wine as blood and bread as flesh. But Matthew, Mark, and Luke were *eye witnesses* to this. But John doesn't mention it at all. In *John* Jesus merely washes his disciples' feet and slyly baits Judas about what he is plotting to do. Did John *forget* about the wine and bread offering? Was he in the bathroom? How do you get stuff like this mixed up?

In *John* Jesus travels about teaching and performing miracles just as in the other Gospels; but two of the miracles in *John* are miracles that the other Gospels never heard of. For example, he changes water into wine at a wedding party, and not only just changes it, but upgrades it to premium quality! Here's the story: At the wedding party, there is consternation among the serving staff because they are running out of wine. Mary asks her son, Jesus, to do something about it. He directs the servants to fill six stone jars with water. Abracadabra! Wine! The servants take the new wine to the steward, who tastes it and is amazed to find it of the highest quality. Rather than being thankful, the steward is appalled that the bridegroom has withheld the good wine until now. 'You're supposed to serve the *good* stuff first,' he scolds, 'while the guests can still appreciate it. You save the cheap wine until last, when they don't care anymore.' (2:12)

But Jesus' most breathtaking miracle by far (aside from his own resurrection) is raising Lazarus from the dead. When Lazarus was still deathly ill, the family, whom Jesus knew well (his friend Mary Magdalene is Lazarus' sister), sent for him. But by the time Jesus arrives Lazarus is already entombed, four days dead. The family warns Jesus against approaching the tomb because by now Lazarus had undoubtedly begun to stink. Yet when Jesus calls for Lazarus to come out, he shuffles forth, still bound in his winding cloth. (11:32-41) Now that is a major miracle. Yet it is not mentioned in *Matthew, Mark* or *Luke*. How is that possible?

Fortunately, the teachings of Jesus in *John* don't conflict with the teachings found in *Mark*, *Matthew* and *Luke*. They don't conflict, but they don't concur either. They're just *other.* Instead of giving a Sermon on the Mount, which basically advises people on how best to manage their mortal affairs, the Jesus of *John* is mostly concerned with convincing as many as he can that he is the Son of God. The concept of the Trinity isn't even touched on in the Synoptic Gospels, but the Jesus of *John* plays it like a harp.

A Whole Different Kind of Jesus
By now we're familiar with the Jesus of the Synoptic Gospels—intelligent, quick-thinking, a wielder at times of threats and at other times golden promises. He is imaginative, skillful with metaphors and capable of luminous eloquence. He's also acutely aware of the political implications of being acclaimed as the Messiah. He carefully skirts the issue, using the ambiguous term "Son of Man" to describe himself. He also tries to dampen down the excitement generated by his miracles, often asking people he's healed not to tell anybody.

Conversely, the Jesus of *John* is supremely confident. He carries himself like the privileged son of an immensely rich father. He knows he's not just an inspired man, but the Spirit *itself*, manifest in the body of Jesus of Nazareth. He's not at all shy about this, to the point of being complacent, even arrogant. Listen to him scolding the Jewish scholars at the Temple:

> *"You are from below;*
> *I am from above.*
> *You are of this world;*
> *I am not of this world.*
> *I have told you already: You will die in your sins.*
> *Yes, if you do not believe that I am He, you will die in your sins."*

8:23-24

The Jesus of the Synoptic Gospels engages the Temple scholars in respectful debate, responding to their arguments with simple but devastating rebuttals. The Jesus of *John* doesn't see the point of entering into a dialogue with such ignoramuses; instead he pounds them with brain-numbing paradoxes, such as:

> *"But as for me, I speak the truth*
> *and for that very reason*
> *you do not believe me."*

8:45

Take *that* little koan back to your cell and wrestle with it.

The Jesus of the Synoptic Gospels treats his listeners like children, soothing them like a parent, scolding them like a parent, frequently using parables—little verbal cartoons—to try to get them to understand what he is saying. The Jesus of *John* doesn't use parables, and his teaching style is more rant than instruction, frequently rising to the level of intense frustration by his listeners' stupidity:

> *"Do you know why you cannot take in what I say?*

> *It is because you are unable to understand my language."*

8:43

Once or twice he just plain goes too far, as in his explanation of the Eucharist, the sacred rite of the transubstantiation of wine into Christ's blood and bread into his flesh. In the Synoptic Gospels, Jesus does it during the Last Supper. The mood is mild, almost convivial. But, remember, John doesn't even mention the first performance of the Eucharist at the Last Supper. But he's a big fan of it now. In fact, he describes the ceremony in such cannibalistic detail that it makes you want to back away:

> *"I tell you most solemnly,*
> *if you do not eat the flesh of the Son of Man*
> *and drink his blood,*
> *you will not have life in you...*
> *For my flesh is real food*
> *and my blood is real drink.*
> *He who eats my flesh and drinks my blood*
> *lives in me*
> *and I live in him."*

6:53-56

The camera swings around to sample the crowd reaction:

> *After hearing it, many of his followers said,*
> *"This is intolerable language. How could*
> *anyone accept it?"*

6:60-61

Aghast, many of them "left him and stopped going with him." (6:66)

You'll remember that in the Synoptic Gospels Jesus is very cautious about letting it get out that he was performing miracles and doing great things in the name of God. Even the usage of words like "Christ" and "Lord" is carefully guarded for fear of prematurely arousing the ire of the Pharisees.

The Jesus of *John*, however, doesn't bother with such precautions. He acts as though he's so full of divinity he can barely hold his shape as a man, much less concern himself with the politics of the day. Here he is in the famous scene in which he meets a Samaritan woman by the well. The disciples have gone into town to buy food and have left him there alone. The woman comes up to draw water, as she has all her life. Jesus asks her for a drink. She delays, teasing him that Jews do not normally ask Samaritans for water (or anything else). And he says,

> *If you only knew what God is offering*
> *and who it is that is saying to you:*
> *Give me a drink,*
> *you would have been the one to ask,*
> *and he would have given you living water.*

4:10

The woman is confused—skeptical, but intrigued. She questions him further, and again he says that the water he gives offers eternal life. Still, she isn't convinced. "I see you are a prophet, sir", she says in tones that are easy to imagine as sarcastic. She then repeats the ancient grievance the Samaritans have against the Jews, over the Jews' insistence that all offerings to God must take place in the Temple at Jerusalem. Jesus replies that soon it will not matter where one worships. The woman, musing, repeats an assurance she has heard since childhood:

> *"I know that Messiah—that is, Christ—is coming; and when he comes he will tell us everything." "I who am speaking to you," said Jesus, "I am he."*

4:25-26

I was struck by that. It seems to me that it takes a lot of nerve to sit by a well in the desert and announce that you are the most towering figure in Jewish history. If I had been that woman I would be backing away, holding my bucket in front of me. That she doesn't says something about the man's charisma.

Your Papers, Please

Two of the criteria for being the Christ are that you must be a direct line descendent of Abraham and David, and that your birthplace is Bethlehem. *Matthew* provides an elaborate genealogy showing that Joseph, Mary's husband, had the required pedigree. *Luke* goes one better, tracing the line back to Adam.

But there's a problem. How can that genealogy possibly apply to Jesus if he didn't have a human father? In order to be descended from Abraham, he has to have some of Abraham's genes. Of course, God being God, He could have put any genes He liked in there. But that seems like cheating, somehow.

Satisfying the other requirement, being born in Bethlehem, is also a tough fit. Jesus' real home town is Nazareth, so getting him born in Bethlehem is going to take some work. *Luke* says that when Mary was pregnant, Caesar ordered a census "of the whole world." Since Joseph was of the house of David, he had to register in a town of that house, and Bethlehem was the closest. It just so happened that while they were there Mary went into labor. Hey, it *could* have happened.

The version in *Matthew* is a little different: there the writer claims that the family was originally from Bethlehem, but had to flee the village because of Herod's decree (unknown to history) that all male infants be killed; eventually they re-settled in Nazareth. *John* never addresses the issue.

The Caiaphas Solution
The dilemma Jesus presents to the Jewish elite hangs over the whole book: if he's crazy—and he seems crazy—they can dismiss him; but if he's not—and sometimes he's scary-smart—he'll dismiss *them*. They just wish he would go away. His popularity is growing, and they know they need to do something. But if they do something and blow it, his popularity will get out of control. On the other hand, if they do nothing, the situation might get out of control anyway. And besides, what if he's the real deal?

The head priest Caiaphas has a clever idea. During a discussion with his colleagues about what to do with Jesus he says:

> *"You don't seem to have grasped the situation at all; you fail to see that it is better for one man to die for the people, than for the whole nation to be destroyed."*

11:49-51

In other words, since Jesus says he's going to sacrifice himself for his people, why not fulfill his prophecy? He'll be gone, we'll be rid of him, and the deluded people who choose to believe in him can be content that his prophecy was fulfilled.

I'm sure it seemed like a good plan at the time, though whenever you create a martyr you're asking for trouble. And they probably were prepared for some martyr-driven backlash. What they didn't realize was that in crucifying Jesus the Jewish authorities not only created a martyr, but they also gave him a chance to perform his greatest miracle, the Resurrection. The Resurrection in turn helped to launch a new religion, Christianity, a spore sac that would eventually spew out hundreds of Christian religions, each of which claims to be the one-and-only official site for salvation.

Acts of the Apostles

Luke ends with the Resurrection. *Acts*, also written by Luke, also addressed to the Roman official Theophilus, takes up the story with Jesus' Ascension:

> *...he was lifted up while* [the Apostles] *looked on, and a cloud took him from their sight.*

1:9-10

Acts is where the New Testament really gets down to business. The Gospels inspired, captivated, and converted us. Now it's time to build on the excitement and create a movement.

The eleven remaining Apostles (12 – Judas = 11) hardly get to take a breath. They are literally still staring up, open-mouthed, at the bright cloud carrying Jesus away when two impatient angels appear. "Why are you men from Galilee standing here looking into the sky?" they say (1:11), and their meaning is clear: 'Get to work!'

The job? Build a religion, and fast, while Jesus' charisma still crackles in the air. The pitch to the masses? Worship this man, follow his teachings, and eternal life will be yours. Judaism, with its lifeless afterworld, its glowering demeanor, its ill-tempered God, isn't one-tenth as sexy. But how to go about the task of forming a new movement isn't clear. The poor Apostles don't even realize they're Christians yet! They thought of themselves as faithful Jews trying to reform their religion. So did Jesus.

What Do We Do Now?
In the first days after Jesus' ascension, the Apostles are in disarray.

They struggle to organize themselves. When the traditional feast of Pentecost[22] arrives, they gather to meet in the same room where the Last Supper occurred. Suddenly,

> *...they heard what sounded like a powerful wind from heaven, the noise of which filled the entire house in which they were sitting; and something appeared to them that seemed like tongues of fire; these separated and came to rest on the head of each of them. They were all filled with the Holy Spirit, and began to speak foreign languages as the Spirit gave them the gift of speech.*

2:1-4

This, of course, is the origin of the practice of "speaking in tongues," a feature of services in many Pentecostal churches. Doing it for the first time, the Apostles make such a racket that a crowd gathers to see what is happening. Some laugh it off. "They have been drinking too much wine," they say. (2:13) Stung, Peter steps forward to refute this, and I love what he says:

> *"These men are not drunk, as you imagine; why, it is only the third hour of the day."*

2:15-16

Of course we're not drunk. It's only nine o'clock in the morning,

---

[22] "Pentecost" (Shavuat in Hebrew) commemorates the anniversary of the day God gave the Torah to the entire nation of Israel assembled at Mt. Sinai. In the Christian tradition it commemorates the descent of the Holy Spirit on the Apostles, which coincides with the Jewish holiday. Thus the two religions celebrate separate events on the same day. It can be confusing!

way too early to start drinking.

Inspiring as it was, this wild Pentecostal visitation doesn't solve the problem of how to form a movement around Jesus' teachings. Remember, for the most part they are fisherman who have been following a charismatic carpenter around Judaea. They probably aren't even literate. Their competitors for the attention of their Jewish brethren are the elite ranks of the Pharisees and the Sadducees. They're at a great disadvantage, and at first things don't go well.

Fast Forward
The first eight chapters cover a period of some years (probably less than ten) as the Apostles, who still regard themselves as Jews, try to recruit followers to their new sect (they never give it a name) and gain legitimacy in the eyes of the Jewish establishment. The Pharisees and the Sadducees, uneasy about this radical new movement, seek to have them suppressed. They have the twelve Apostles arrested (5:17) and brought before the high court, whose members are uncertain what to do with them. The Apostles haven't actually done anything wrong, aside from some noisy proselytizing, but on the other hand they are a real annoyance. In a hedging, blurry verdict, the officials decide that the Christ followers are entitled to their beliefs, but not entitled to preach them. The Apostles proclaim that they will preach as much as they like, but the court chooses to ignore that. They are sentenced to a light flogging and released.

This uneasy truce begins to unwind when one of the faithful, Stephen, goes too far: "…filled with grace and power [he] began to work miracles and great signs among the people." (6:8-9) He is accused of blasphemy, and brought before the high court. Toward the end of a long speech in his own defense, he steps over the line:

> *But Stephen, filled with the Holy Spirit, gazed into heaven.... "I can see heaven thrown open," he said, "and the Son of Man standing at the right hand of God."*

7:55-57

That is too much for the judges.

> *At this all the members of the council shouted out and stopped their ears with then hands; then they all rushed at him, sent him out of the city and stoned him.*

7:57-58

That is, *stoned until dead.* Standing as an approving witness to the stoning, in fact watching over the pile of cloaks shed by the mob, is a young Jewish militant named Saul, who soon will be calling himself Paul.

The Perils of Paul

Paul appears on the Biblical scene five to ten years after the ascension of Jesus. He was raised as an orthodox Jew. In the early part of his career he was called Saul, and was known as a fierce enemy of the new sect that was proclaiming Jesus as the Christ. Armed with letters of marque from the high priest, he traveled around Judaea, beating and arresting followers of the Jesus sect and sending them back to Jerusalem for judgment.

On his way to Damascus to persecute the Christians there, Saul is ambushed by Jesus, who speaks to him out of a "light from heaven." Saul is usually pictured as falling from his donkey at this moment, thumping blinded to the ground, though no animal is mentioned in the text. "Saul, Saul," says a voice in the light, "why are you persecuting me?" "Who are you, Lord?" Saul asks. "I am Jesus, and you are persecuting me." (9:4-6)

Jesus then tells Saul to continue on to Damascus and await further orders. Saul, now blind, is helped on his way by his companions. When he arrives in the city, a follower of Jesus named Ananias, whom God has instructed to seek Saul out, lays his hands upon Saul and restores his sight. Saul must feel somewhat shell-shocked by now, but no matter; the important thing is that he's a believer, and he's about to become the most fearless and productive proselytizer in history.

Saul, Paul?
Saul's father is a Roman citizen. His son has two names, his Jewish one (Saul) and his Roman one (Paul). Soon after Saul/Paul accepts Jesus as the Christ, he starts using his Roman name, Paul, which emphasizes his Roman citizenship which, in turn, allows him to travel more freely within the Roman Empire than if he were simply a citizen of Judea. Also, he can demand and receive protection from local Roman authorities.

Born in Tarsus (a coastal city located in what is today Turkey), Paul has a more cosmopolitan perspective than the provincial Apostles, who never seem to stray from Jerusalem. Though he considers himself a Jew (but not for long) he has credibility with the gentile (pagan) community that the Jewish Apostles could never hope to have.

Peter Preaches to the Gentiles
Right about this time (ca. 35 or 36 CE), Peter, who is clearly the leader among the Apostles, makes an important breakthrough. He has a vision in which a voice from heaven instructs him to eat meat that orthodox Jews would consider unclean. He protests, but the

voice says, "What God has made clean, you have no right to call profane." (10:15-16) This is the first sliver of doctrinal difference between traditional Jewish practice and the observances of Jesus' followers. More is to come.

A Roman centurion named Cornelius asks Peter to come to his house and talk about the teachings of Jesus, and Peter agrees. This is a big deal. Jews were forbidden to mix with gentiles, and here Paul is *preaching* to them. These Roman pagans are so inspired by the sermon that they too are filled with the Holy Spirit and begin speaking in tongues. Peter orders them to be baptized (10:48), and with that, a line has been crossed. The Jews led by the Apostles have set themselves apart from the traditional Jews by agreeing to accept pagans into their community.

Some of these Jewish followers of Jesus Christ begin to feel threatened. Following the uproar over Stephen's stoning (see above), some flee Judaea. A group settles in Antioch (located in what is today southern Turkey) and begins to preach to their gentile Greek neighbors. Wanting to set themselves apart from traditional Jews, they call themselves "Christians."

Paul, the First Missionary
While the Apostles huddle in Jerusalem, endlessly dickering with the Jewish establishment, Paul single-handedly sets out to bring Jesus' teachings to the greater world. His plan is brilliant: *convert the pagans*. The pagan market is much bigger than the fraction of Jews that are willing to listen to the Apostles, and the pagans are not nearly as suspicious. Paul enlists the gospel writer Luke as his secretary and personal historian, and the two set off to bring the Good News[23] to the wider world.

Paul's first stop is Antioch, which he makes his de facto home base. Without seeking permission from the Apostles in Jerusalem, he launches himself at the world, Christianity's first wild-eyed missionary to the pagans. For at least fourteen years (and probably more), he travels with various companions (always including Luke) throughout Asia Minor, spreading the Word. The length and breadth of his peregrinations is breathtaking: Cyprus, Crete, Athens, Thessalonika…the list goes on and on.

Paul develops a modus operandi: when he arrives in a city, he visits the synagogue and asks permission to speak to the congregation. Sometimes the rabbis agree to that, sometimes they don't. What almost always happens is that once Paul starts speaking, his listeners are appalled. Not only does he want to treat gentiles as equals before God, but he's also maintains that they don't have to follow Torah law! 'You don't have to be circumcised,' he tells his listeners. 'You can eat unclean food.' The Jews are outraged. *'Why, this man is not a Jew at all!'* Then they throw him out.

Then Paul, unfazed, goes out into the city at large and begins preaching to the pagans, who are generally more receptive. His simple message—repent, accept Jesus, and eternal life is yours—is seductive, and people buy into it. He organizes a Christian congregation, establishes a church, and hangs around until the converts learn how to run their religion.

At some point, the Jews of the city come after him. At the very least they chase him out of town. Often they beat him first. Occasionally, they throw him in jail and put him on trial as a

---

[23] The word *gospel* derives from the Old English *gōd-spell*, meaning "good news" or "glad tidings"

blasphemer. One way or another, he always beats the rap (this is where being a Roman citizen comes in handy). Then he goes on to the next city. This scenario, with variations, is replayed over and over again.

Finally, the Apostles in Jerusalem get wind of what's going on. They send a group of disciples to Antioch to apply corrective instruction to the newly-minted Christians. Here is what they say:

> *"Unless you have yourselves circumcised in the tradition of Moses you cannot be saved."*

15:1-2

Now it's Paul's turn to be outraged. He argues with the members of the Jerusalem task force, to no avail. Finally, they all agree that Paul should go to Jerusalem and have it out with the Apostles.

First Apostolic Council
Paul's showdown with the Apostles is now called the First Apostolic Council. It occurred somewhere around 50 CE. It is one of those watershed moments. The record of what actually went on appears to be heavily redacted. Surely the proceedings were more tempestuous than the mild exchange reported in Chapter 15. At issue is whether the pagans converted by Paul are Jews or…something else. In any case, a compromise is forged. The Apostle James issues this finding:

> *"I rule, then, that instead of making things more difficult for pagans who turn to God, we send them a letter telling them merely to abstain from anything polluted by idols, from fornication, from the meat of strangled animals, and from blood."*

15:19-21

This is an astonishing statement. The Apostles must have been desperate hold onto Paul's congregations because here they have stretched Jewish law to the limit and beyond.

Just *look* at what Paul walks away with: if his Christians agree not to worship idols, to refrain from sex between unmarried persons, and accept the extremely modified dietary restrictions, *they can still call themselves Jews!* They don't even have to be circumcised! (Abraham must have been spinning in his grave.) That's it. Accept Jesus, follow these easy rules, and you're just as saved as the Apostles themselves.

The calving off of the Christian religion from the glacier of Judaism is almost complete. Not quite yet, though. Paul's "Christians" are still technically Jews.

On the Road Again
With this victory under his belt, Paul goes back on the road, running his one-man show. He resumes visiting cities, starting up a churches, causing riots, getting beaten, jailed, and (as a Roman citizen) released. And then he does it again, and again, and again…

There is one amusing encounter with the intellectual snobs in Athens. Every day Paul goes into the city's marketplace and engages in debate with anyone who cares to talk to him.

> *Even a few Epicurean and Stoic philosophers argued with him. Some said, "Does this parrot know what he's talking about?…He sounds like a propagandist for some outrageous gods."*

17:18

Finally, Paul is invited to speak before the Athenian high court of appeal, the Council of Areopagus. This promises to be a good show because, as the text says, "The one amusement the Athenians and the foreigners living there seem to have, apart from discussing the latest ideas, is listening to lectures about them." (17:21)

Predictably, the Athenians find Paul more entertaining than credible. When he begins to explain how Jesus rose from the dead, "some of them burst out laughing." (17:32) Obviously, no Christian church was going to be established in Athens, not even in a strip mall.

Arrest and Trial in Jerusalem
After a few more years on the road, Paul decides it's time to return to Jerusalem and renew contact with to the Apostles. Here is where his real troubles begin. The orthodox Jews loathe Paul, and they jump at this opportunity to attack him. The Apostles aren't his biggest fans either. They've never wholly forgiven him for bringing pagans into their faith. True, Peter established the precedent, but surely his idea was to *tolerate* pagans, not *recruit* them. In any event, the Apostles quietly decline to come to Paul's defense as his crisis with the orthodox Jewish establishment deepens.

Soon the orthodox Jews stage a full-scale riot against Paul, intending to seize him and kill him on the spot. Determined to restore order, the Roman tribune stationed in Jerusalem takes Paul into protective custody. In 22:24 the tribune orders Paul to be put to the lash in order to extract an explanation for why the people want to kill him. But Paul pulls out his Roman ID and immediately the effusively apologetic tribune removes Paul's chains. Nevertheless, he requires Paul to appear before the full council of Jewish elders called the Sanhedrin. Again a riot threatens to break out, and the tribune hurriedly takes Paul back into the Roman stronghold places him under protective custody. He makes arrangements to transfer Paul to the next highest level of Roman authority—the governor of Judea.

"A Perfect Pest"

The governor, whose name is Felix, agrees to conduct a trial. He assigns a Roman prosecutor named Tertullus to represent the Jewish plaintiffs. Here is the prosecutor giving his opening statement:

> *"The plain truth is that we find this man a perfect pest; he stirs up trouble among Jews the world over and is a ringleader of the Nazarene sect.*

24:5

A perfect pest! To Paul's ears that would have been a compliment.

Representing himself in the defense, Paul's opening statement is succinct and elegant:

> *"As you can verify for yourself, it is no more than twelve days since I sent up to Jerusalem on pilgrimage, and it is not true that they ever found me arguing with anyone or stirring up the mob, either in the Temple, in the synagogues, or about the town; neither can they prove any of the accusations they are making against me now."*

24:11-21

And so the courtroom drama begins. I'm not going to go into all the details, but basically, after listening to the arguments, Felix adjourns the trial until further notice, and puts Paul back into protective custody (presumably, as a Roman citizen, Paul is given comfortable accommodations even though he is confined). The truth is, Felix has no intention of rendering a judgment himself, which would result in an uproar no matter which side he came down on. He waits two years until his term as governor is up, and hands the problem to his replacement, Porcius Festus.

When the trial resumes, Festus, wishing to get this politically explosive problem off his desk, proposes to turn Paul over to the Jewish court in Jerusalem. Paul, knowing this would surely seal his doom, invokes his right as a Roman citizen to be tried in Rome before Caesar. Festus agrees.

The trip to Rome by ship is a hair-raising adventure, taking more than three months. But in the end Paul arrives in Rome to await his fate. He is put under house arrest and for two years lives in relative comfort.

And then…Paul disappears from the Bible. History does not record what Caesar, who by now was crucifying Christians left and right, did with Paul. Most everyone agrees that he was probably crucified.

But what a bequest he left behind!

The Letters of Saint Paul

Christians had their charismatic figure in Jesus. The movement was growing. There were plenty of Christians. The problem was there was no *Christianity*. The movement needed structure. It needed doctrine, dogma and, above all, congregations and Sunday collections. It needed Paul, the man who invented Christianity.

The Letters of Saint Paul—the next fourteen books of the Bible—are the heart of the New Testament. In them, Paul imparts how, in order to be good Christians, people were to behave in their daily lives. What's fascinating is that Paul puts the Christian faith together on the fly, improvising the rules as he addressed problems arising within the early congregations.

Until Paul, to qualify as an Apostle you had to be someone who had personally known and traveled with Jesus, someone the Master had specifically enlisted to go out and spread the Gospel. Paul was different. He never knew Jesus personally. Paul's claim to being an Apostle was based solely on a purely mystical and private confrontation he had with Jesus' spirit on the road to Damascus. It did not necessarily go down well with the established Apostles when this famous persecutor of Jews came thundering in from Asia Minor saying "I'm an Apostle too!"

But Paul had a couple of advantages. He loved to argue—he was indefatigable—and he was a Roman citizen, a fact that gave him a tremendous advantage as a spreader of the Gospel because it gave him the freedom to travel at will throughout the empire.

Before Paul, the work of spreading the Gospel was going at a snail's pace. Peter, James, John and the rest of the blue ribbon

Apostles were Jerusalem-bound xenophobes. They believed that all of Jesus' teaching applied first to the Chosen People and then maybe, way down the line, to some of the virtuous pagans in the world. So they stayed in Jerusalem and went to the synagogue with orthodox Jews and tried to influence them into accepting Jesus as the Christ. That was as far as their imagination could take them.

But Paul, who didn't feel tied to Jerusalem, saw that the real constituency, the real market for Christianity was among the people he felt more comfortable with anyway—the Greeks and the Romans and all their various subjected peoples. The Apostles could take care of Jerusalem. Paul set his sights on the rest of the world.

At first the Apostles were only too glad to let him do as he pleased. It wasn't forbidden to preach to the gentiles, just...a tiny bit irrelevant. Only after a few years had passed, and it became clear that Paul's work in Syria, Turkey and Greece was creating a large population of people who called themselves Christians (the term was coined by the faithful in Antioch), did Peter and James and the rest become concerned.

That's when Paul was ordered back to Jerusalem, to face what is now called the First Apostolic Council, which was held to resolve the question of whether or not uncircumcised people are acceptable to God. As we saw in *Acts,* Paul's victory was almost absolute. The way was cleared for him convert pagans to Christianity without them having to obey most of Torah law. In effect, you didn't have to become a Jew to be a Christian.

"As a result," Paul wrote to the Christian congregation at Galatia, "these people who are acknowledged leaders—not that their importance matters to me, since God has no favorites—these leaders, as I say, had nothing to add to the Good News as I preach it." [Galatians 2:6-7]

So Paul was left free to manage his churches as he saw fit, both in person and through letters. As he wrote them, responding to crises, clarifying doctrinal questions, he invented Christian theology. If you read them in the chronological order, you can see the complexity of his thought accumulating.

More than anywhere else in the Bible, *The Letters of Saint Paul* give you the sense that you are dealing with a single, strong personality.

The fourteen Pauline letters are, according to scholars, of varying authenticity, ranging from Paul's undoubted authorship of *1 Thessalonians*, *1* and *2 Corinthians, Galatians, Romans, Phillipians* and *Philemon* to his mere influence over most of the other letters. There is a convention about the composition, which is that Paul is dictating his thoughts to a faithful scribe who is writing as fast as he can.

A couple of issues dominate Paul's thinking, especially early in his career. Foremost is his belief that Jesus is going to return in his lifetime. According to how Paul understood it, the world had between now and when Jesus returned (any moment, but surely within a few years) to accept him as the Son of God. Those that have not accepted him by then would be damned forever. Paul's early letters burn with the urgency of this belief and the duty of haste it imposes on him.

The other essential issue for Paul was to define just what true acceptance is. Traditional Jewish thinking, including that of the

Apostles, held that virtue in God's eyes was simultaneously secured and demonstrated by adherence to the Law—that grim and bizarre body of precepts passed down through the Mosaic tradition. In addition to that, the Apostles also believed that Jesus was the Messiah that the old literature had promised would come. They saw no conflict between the Law and their faith in Jesus. But Paul believed that the appearance of Jesus upon the earth rendered the Law obsolete.

Essentially his argument was this: Since God sent His only Son to die for our sins, the time of the Law is over. Jewish history as told in the Old Testament proves that by themselves men cannot live up to God's standards. God conceded that point, and sent his son Jesus Christ to sacrifice himself for mankind's sins. Grace is now achieved by the simple act of accepting the gift of Jesus' sacrifice. That's it. Nothing else is required. There is no test for it. Only you and Jesus (when He returns, soon, *soon*) will know whether or not you've accepted Him.

But if you think that was enough to satisfy a continent full of gentile Christians, you're wrong. They had plenty of questions and doubts. The Thessalonians wanted to know, for example, what happened to members of their congregation who died before Jesus returned. Were they out of luck, or was He going to save them too? That question (and others) earned the Thessalonians two letters from Paul

These sorts of problems cropped up over and over. While Paul was spending two years with the Ephesians, the Galatian church was going to hell in a handcar. The resulting letter to the Galatians was Paul's attempt to exert his authority over them and set them back on the right path.

We'll go into the letters in more detail below.

So, for about thirty years Paul raced back and forth across Asia Minor visiting various congregations and writing letters to the others, laboring tirelessly to keep the fledgling religion alive. He did pretty well too. There is no question that by the time Paul was placed under arrest—about 65 CE—and sent to Rome, he was at the head of a very impressive religious movement indeed.

Here is Paul preaching:

> *"For Christ did not send me to baptize, but to preach the Good News, and not to preach that in the terms of philosophy, in which the crucifixion of Christ cannot be expressed. The language of the cross may be illogical to those who are not on the way to salvation, but those of us who are on the way see it as God's power to save. As scripture says:* ***I shall destroy the wisdom of the wise and bring to nothing all the learning of the learned.***[24] *Where are the philosophers now? Where are the scribes? Where are any of our thinkers today? Do you see now how God has shown up the foolishness of human wisdom? If it was God's wisdom that human wisdom should not know God, it was because God wanted to save those who have faith through the foolishness of the message that we preach."*

1 Corinthians 1:17-21

---

[24] A paraphrase of *Isaiah* 29:14.

You cannot be saved by thinking alone. In fact, thinking gets in the way. To a philosopher this message sounds foolish, but Paul is warning that only the "foolish" will be saved.

But Paul breaks his own rule all the time. He had so much confidence in his ability to logically defend his faith that he actually took up a spot in the market place of Athens (*Acts* 17) and engaged all comers in debate, including "a few Epicurean and Stoic philosophers..." Unfortunately he was laughed out of town, but the fact that he even tried says something about his pride.

Paul writes with a conversational directness that's entirely new in the Bible: Here he is discussing whether it is necessary to be celibate to be a good Christian:

> *"I have no directions from the Lord but give my own opinion as one who, by the Lord's mercy, has stayed faithful. Well then, I believe that in these present times of stress this is right: that it is good for a man to stay as he is. If you are tied to a wife, do not look for freedom; if you are free of a wife, then do not look for one. But if you marry, it is no sin, and it is not a sin for a young girl to get married. They will have their troubles, though, in their married life, and I should like to spare you that."*

1 Cor. 25-28

"If you are tied to a wife, do not look for freedom." Women as tar babies. If you're stuck to one, it's better not to struggle. If you're free don't even think about getting stuck. I guess we know what Paul thought of marriage. Don't you love it when a priest gives you marital advice?

Now, quickly, we are going to skim over the letters one by one, in the chronological order in which scholars have arranged them:

1 Thessalonians

The Thessalonian congregation had some very basic questions, such as what is going to happen to those of them who have died before Jesus returns. They were expecting to meet Jesus in person, after all, and for the dead it seems to be too late.

Paul's answer is brief and direct:

> *"...those who have died in Christ will be the first to rise, and then those of us who are still alive will be taken up in the clouds, together with them, to meet the Lord in the air."*

4:16-17

Not only to you get to meet him, you don't even lose your place in line.

2 Thessalonians

This letter addresses the question of when the faithful can expect to be gathered up and transported to heaven. In his answer Paul reaches back to the apocalyptic tradition of Daniel to come up with some smoking signs and portents. It's comic book writing, as if Paul is drawing a picture for these stubborn, dull children:

> *"It cannot happen until the Great Revolt has taken place and the Rebel, the Lost One, has appeared. This is the Enemy, the one who claims...that he is God. The Lord will kill him with the breath of His mouth and will annihilate him with his glorious appearance at His coming.*

2:3-8

He could have just said, "I don't know."

1 Corinthians
The Corinthians were probably Paul's most troublesome flock. Corinth was the Hong Kong of its time, a seaport, the richest and most populous city in Greece. The Corinthian faithful were quick to question Paul's authority, quick to break into feuding factions. Judging from the questions and problems Paul responds to in his two letters to them, the Corinthians (at least some of them) were as interested in exploiting the new religion as in being saved by it. They are like naughty children, trying to figure out how to get around the rules.

The petty (and not so petty) problems the Corinthians raise force Paul to new doctrinal heights. Here are some of the issues he addresses:

> **Fornication.** By "fornication" Paul means sex outside of marriage, even between two unmarried people. And of course you shouldn't do it. The woman partner is, of course, no better than a prostitute. The man is…well, just a man. *"You know, surely, that your bodies are members making up the body of Christ; do you think I can take parts of Christ's body and join them to the body of a prostitute?"* (6:15-16)
>
> **Marriage and Virginity.** Celibacy is best. Marriage is the best protection for those who cannot be celibate. (7:1-3)

Divorce. It is permissible only if the offending partner is not a believer and refuses to tolerate the practices of the believing partner. (7:15)

Eating Food Sacrificed to Idols. Shrugging off the ruling of the First Apostolic Council, Paul says go ahead, since the idols have no meaning, but only if it doesn't disturb someone else. This was a trickier issue than it seems. The pleasure-loving Corinthians knew that only the best cuts got offered up to the gods, after which the picked-over meat was sold in the marketplace. Thus, for some of these newly-minted Christians, being given permission to eat pagan meat was a definite plus. It was a tricky issue for Paul to weigh. True, the meat was not tainted in God's eyes, since the other deities did not exist, but Paul was afraid that if one Christian saw another Christian eating meat previously offered to a pagan god it might confuse the one whose faith was weaker. Best not to eat any meat at all. (8:7-13)

Communion. Apparently some of the Corinthian congregation had taken to regarding Communion as an actual meal. It was, after all, the Lord's Last Supper they were celebrating. So they were coming to church on Sunday with hearty appetites, impatient to eat. When the time came for this most sacred of the Church's rites there was an unseemly rush for the bread and wine. Some people were getting none and others were getting drunk. With a mild reprimand ("I cannot congratulate you for this") and the patience of an elementary school teacher, Paul reminds the congregation that the Lord's Supper is a ritual, not a meal, and suggests that people who are hungry should eat at home first, before coming to church. (11:17-34)

The Gift of Tongues. Crying out in church in an unknown foreign tongue was an easy way to show that God was in your body, and fun besides. But it must have been getting out of hand, because Paul here gently lays out an elaborate etiquette for the practice. Here is part of it:

> *If there are people present with the gift of tongues, let only two or three, at the most, be allowed to use it, and only one at a time, and there must be someone to interpret.*

14:27-28

Resurrection of the Dead. The more years that passed without Jesus returning, the more the piling-up dead were becoming a problem for Paul. He's already assured the Thessalonians that their dead would be taken care of. Here he refines that teaching, explaining that bodies don't go to heaven, only spirits. So the death of the body signifies nothing:

> *"Flesh and blood cannot inherit the kingdom of God: and the perishable cannot inherit what lasts forever. I will tell you something that has been secret: that we are not all going to die, but we shall all be changed. This will be instantaneous, in the twinkling of an eye, when the last trumpet sounds. It will sound, and the dead will be raised, imperishable..."*
> 15:52-53

This raises a theological question that is still being debated in some circles. Paul seems to be saying that only the soul is taken to heaven (at least, nothing of flesh and blood). But in *Ezekiel* 37:5-7 we read:

> *The Lord Yahweh says this to these bones: "I am now going to make the breath enter you, and you will live. I shall put sinews on you, I shall make flesh grown on you, I shall cover you with skin and give you breath, and you will live; and you will learn that I am Yahweh."*

Paul says no to bodies, Yahweh says yes to bodies. Sorting out stuff like this is what divinity schools are for.

Sunday Collection. No matter is too small for Paul's doctrinal wand. Here he says that each person should contribute at least something every Sunday. For Paul, this was a fairly trivial matter, just a question of raising money for the poor in Jerusalem. But over time the practice of collecting money every Sunday will raise billions and billions of dollars and make the Catholic Church one of the most powerful institutions ever invented.

Fornication. Coming to church hungry. The gift of tongues. This is how an institution grows up, isn't it? Not by retaining a management consultant and poring over flow-charts, but by solving problems one at a time, as they come up.

2 Corinthians Finally, the Corinthians manage to push Paul too far. Apparently what has happened is that in Paul's absence someone has approached the congregation and suggested that as an Apostle, Paul is a lightweight, that he writes tough letters but is a coward in person, that he imposes no real discipline on his followers, and that the fact that he takes no money shows that he knows he isn't worth much. In response, Paul throws the gauntlet down:[25]

---

[25] Most scholars agree that *2 Corinthians* is a compilation of two letters, maybe more. Thus, Paul's angry rant consumes chapters 10-13, and the more conciliatory aftermath fills chapters 1-9. No, it doesn't make sense, but there it is.

> *"Someone* [among you] *said, 'He writes powerful and strongly worded letters but when he is with you, you see only half a man and no preacher at all.' The man who said that can remember this: whatever we are like in the words of our letters when we are absent, that is what we shall be like in our actions when we are present."*

10:9-11

Changing the mood, he inserts a melodramatic résumé of his sufferings on their behalf:

> *"...five times I have had the thirty-nine lashes from the Jews; three times I have been beaten with sticks; once I was stoned, three times I have been shipwrecked..."*
> 11:24-25

Finally he comes to the heart of the matter:

> *"What I am afraid of is that when I come I may find you different from what I want you to be, and you may find that I am not as you would like me to be; and then there will be wrangling, jealousy, and tempers roused, intrigues and backbiting and gossip, obstinacies and disorder. I am afraid that on my next visit, my God may make me ashamed on your account... This will be the third time I have come to you. The evidence of three, or at least two, witnesses is necessary to sustain the charge. I gave warning when I was with you the second time*

> *and I give warning now, too… when I come again, I shall have no mercy."*

12:20-21, 13:1-3

He's playing Moses here, Yahweh in human form. The Corinthians, if they have
any remnant of credulous attachment to Paul, have got to be clutching their robes and wondering what they should do now.

Don't Worry, I Still Love You
In Chapters 1-9 Paul in a much more relenting mood. Obviously, the storm has passed. The leader of the rebellion (who is never identified) has been excommunicated (literally thrown out of the community). Paul actually seems a little ashamed of the rhetorical excesses his rage drove him to. "If we seemed out of our senses, it was for God; but if we are being reasonable now, it is for your sake." (5:13) This is written from Macedonia, from whence he's writing to say he's decided not to make a return visit to Corinth after all ('WHEW!' thinks the battered little church), and that maybe it's time to think in terms of Christian forgiveness. "The punishment already imposed by the majority on the man in question is enough; and the best thing now is to give him your forgiveness and encouragement, or he might break down from so much misery." (2:6-8)

Looking back on the incident, though, Paul does not regret any suffering he may have caused. "Yours has been a kind of suffering that God approves, and so you have come to no kind of harm from us....Just look at what suffering in God's way has brought you: what keenness, what explanations, what indignation, what alarm!" (7:9-11)

But now to get on with the business of this letter. Don't think he doesn't know he's got the Corinthians by the short hairs. A good time, then, to formalize the practice of the Sunday collection. Paul begins by professing to be astonished at the generosity of the Macedonian congregation when it comes to sending money to the poor brothers in Jerusalem. Now watch him put the squeeze on the Corinthians:

> *"You always have the most of everything—of faith, of eloquence, of understanding, of keenness for any cause, and the biggest share of our affection—so we expect you to put the most into this work of mercy too. It is not an order that I am giving you; I am just testing the genuineness of your love against the keenness of others."*
> 8:7-9

He goes on for fully a page like this, twisting and squeezing and screwing it to them. No Jewish mother ever provoked guilt more skillfully to exact miserable obedience. And no politician ever anticipated his constituency's suspicious nature more suavely when it comes to money matters. At the end of all this he has the nerve to close by saying that he's really not trying to put pressure on them, but just to "make sure that the gift you promised is all ready, and that it all comes as a gift out of your generosity and not by being extorted from you."

I'm *sure!*

Shedding the Old Testament
One other thing comes up in *2 Corinthians* that shouldn't be overlooked, and that is the beginning of Paul's campaign against the Old Testament. It's a tricky business, because he has to pretend

to be genuflecting to it even as he is shoving it out of the way. The Old Testament Law, in his view, provides the background that proves the authenticity of Jesus' claim to be the Christ. The prophecies about the Messiah are there; the proof of God's intervention in Jewish history is there.

As a guide to living, however, Paul believes the Law should be put aside. Jewish history is the history of a people who could not keep to the Law. In Paul's view, the gap between the Law and its observance is a measurement of the vastness of the people's sinfulness; sin so deep that they could not recognize their Savior when he came, and so killed him. The point is that, from Paul's perspective, the Law and the tradition it held together were a kind of holding tank to keep the word of God alive until the prophecies could be fulfilled. Now that Jesus has come (and gone) the Law is an empty shell, and the people who still cling to it (including the Christian brothers in Jerusalem) are wrongheaded.

Paul recalls a detail from that part of *Exodus* that deals with Moses and the first days of the Law. The narrative describes Moses' face becoming so blindingly bright after his meeting with Yahweh that the Israelites couldn't stand to be with him unless he wore a veil. Whenever Moses went to speak with Yahweh he would take down the veil.

> *"And when he came out, he would tell the sons of Israel what he had been ordered to pass on to them, and the sons of Israel would see the face of Moses radiant. Then Moses would put the veil back over his face until he returned to speak with Yahweh."*

That's from *Exodus 34:35* and that's all that book has to say on the matter. Paul has something to add, however. He claims that though at first Moses' face was too bright to look at, it was a brightness that inevitably faded, and that Moses wore the veil "so that the Israelites would not notice the ending of what had to fade." (3:13-14)

To me that's a pernicious piece of propaganda; a cold-blooded revision of a history that his gentile readers don't know well enough to question. Having established the historical "fact" of Moses' fading face, Paul goes on to employ it in a skillful weaving of rhetoric and metaphor:

> *"And anyway, their minds had been dulled; indeed, to this very day, that same veil is still there when the old covenant is being read, a veil never lifted, since Christ alone can remove it. Yes, even today, whenever Moses is read, the veil is over their minds. It will not be removed until they turn to the Lord. Now this Lord is the Spirit, and where the Spirit of the Lord is, there is freedom. And we, with our unveiled faces reflecting like mirrors the brightness of the Lord, all grow bright as we are turned into the image that we reflect; this is the work of the Lord who is Spirit."*

3:14-18

Hoo boy, that's a preacher cookin' and a damn good one. A good preacher, but not an overly scrupulous man.

Galatians

Often Paul's letters are directed back to a congregation he has just left, written out of his concern that in his absence their faith will waver. He sometimes gets reports while he's on the road that they're abusing their new freedoms, that they're listening to the Jewish critics, and he worries that he's losing them. It really is a testimony to the power of this man's personality that he was able to hold these widely disparate groups to his view. Because it *is* a radical view, way beyond what Jesus himself preached. Jesus was a Jew. He saw himself as the culmination of Jewish prophecies that promised a new leader from the line of David. He told his followers to save Jews first and gentiles second, if at all.

But Paul was saying, 'Forget all that. That's not what Jesus really meant. The real message, which I have received directly from Jesus by revelation, is that when he rose from the dead, the Law died; being a good Jew is no longer the path to salvation.' Who would have thought that somebody preaching such a radical line would be the winner of the What Is Our Doctrine contest?

The secret of Paul's success is easy enough to see now—he identified a newer, much larger market for his product, and went after it with fanatic determination. The more traditional-minded sales managers, i.e. the Apostles, were aware that the market was there, but they regarded it with distaste and were reluctant to approach it—preaching the Christ, the Savior, to the uncircumcised? Yuk! So when Paul won the battle for the gentile market, he won the war over who would write Christian doctrine.

It is in his letter to the Galatians that he first comes straight out and says the Law is no longer relevant. The letter is prompted, of course, by the predictable wavering of the faith in his absence. Aside from the pressure of Jewish Christians who want to make sure that the Law and Christian faith stay knitted together, there are those among the Galatians who feel that following some Jewish practices might be a good idea; agreeing to circumcision, for example, without troubling to follow the dietary and cleansing laws.

To those tempted by this suggestion Paul says, "Are you people in Galatia mad?" (3:1) and "I would like to see the knife slip." (5:12) He thinks the preoccupation with circumcision is silly, and sillier yet those who would have the surgery performed without pledging to follow the Law it symbolizes.

So what did Paul think the Law was good for? Was he rejecting its place in history as well as in the New Age? In *Galatians* he addresses the question straight on:

> *"What then was the purpose of adding the Law? This was done to specify crimes, until the posterity came to whom the promise was addressed."*
> 3:19

The Law served the purpose of holding things together—"to specify crimes"—until Jesus came. The generation that saw him is "the posterity...to whom the promise was addressed." As soon as Jesus appeared, the Law became invalid and irrelevant. Here is the crucial passage in Paul's campaign to liberate Christians of the Law's impossible burden, the moment when the jeweler's hammer taps down and creates a fissure that can't be resealed:

> *"Though we were born as Jews and not pagan sinners, we acknowledge that what makes a man righteous is not obedience to the Law, but faith in Jesus Christ. We had to become believers in Christ Jesus no less than you* [gentiles] *had, and now we hold that faith in*

> *Christ rather than fidelity to the Law is what justifies us, and that no one can be justified by keeping to the Law."*

2:15-21

Peter, James, and John must have gone nuts when they read that. Paul's *Letter to the Galations* is a declaration of war against the Law, the beginning of a full-fledged schismatic death struggle over who are Jesus' true heirs.

Guess who won?

Romans

Most of Paul's letters really are *letters*. They are addressed to specific congregations or sometimes individual people. *Romans* is different. It is a letter mainly by convention, by its adherence to the epistolary form. Because the church in Rome was not one that Paul had founded, he didn't feel as attached to it as to his own churches, and it shows in the more dignified, formal tone of this letter. It is a formal position paper explaining Christian doctrine as Paul saw it.

At a deliberate pace, in closely reasoned statements, *Romans* traces over the same doctrinal territory covered by *Galatians*:

> *"Well then, sin entered the world through one man [Adam], and through sin death, and thus death has spread through the whole human race because everyone has sinned."*
> 5:12-13

That is the basic condition, the default setting. Law or no law, circumcision or no circumcision, we're all in that boat together.

And nothing we can do is within our powers as human beings can change that. Only God can intervene in this perpetuation of misery.

This is the doctrine, in case you hadn't recognized it, of Original Sin, and though it had been hanging there like a ripe fruit for centuries, no Jewish prophet or Christian apostle had until this moment seized it and held it up like this.

> *"I cannot understand my own behavior. I fail to carry out the things I want to do, and I find myself doing the very things I hate.... The fact is, I know of nothing good living in me—living, that is, in my unspiritual self—for though the will to do what is good is in me, the performance is not, with the result that instead of doing the good things I want to do, I carry out the sinful things I do not want. When I act against my will, then, it is not my true self doing it, but sin which lives in me."*

7:15-20

Thanks to Paul, I suppose, that passage does not seem that alien to me; it's not unlike the criticism I levy against myself every day. This kind of sour, self-denigrating assessment of oneself is one of Paul's many contributions to Western thinking about the nature of man.

But not everything Paul says goes down so smoothly. Our sense of right and wrong is gives us clues as to how God wants us to behave, and to that extent it's useful. Rut when it comes to forming an opinion of God's actions, Paul is quite clear that the human sense of right and wrong has no place.

> *"But what right have you, a human being, to cross-examine God? 'The pot has no right to say to the potter: Why did you make me this shape?' Surely a potter can do what he likes with the clay? It is surely for him to decide whether he will use a particular lump of clay to make a special pot or an ordinary one?"*

9:20-21

We're too low a life form to judge God's actions and decisions. Human merit has nothing to do with saving the soul. God's grace and condemnation fall on whomever he pleases, regardless of their blame- or praise-worthiness. And if you insist on defying that, relying, for example, on what your sense of right and wrong tells you in order to conduct yourself as best you know how, you might as well get in the coal-car with the rest of the damned.

Get in that coal car because, as Paul demonstrated by examining his own behavior, even when the human sense of right and wrong sorts things out properly, as often as not we can't make ourselves do what we know we should do anyway.

Now the next step in Paul's campaign to erase right behavior as a component of salvation: "...God's choice is free, since it depends on the one who calls, not on human merit." (9:12) That is, humans cannot limit God's choices by insisting he pick out only the good ones. One is saved by grace, "...nothing therefore to do with good deeds, or grace would not be grace at all!" (11:6) A gift is a gift, you cannot earn it.

The Author's Two Cents

This aspect of Christian doctrine has always left me scratching my head. How can we *not* be judged by our actions? Actions—and even thoughts are actions—are how we express our existence. Assessing the good and evil of my actions are how I judge myself. I can't accept that God would do any less. That's the essence of hubris, I suppose, thinking that I know what God's standards should be. Paul's rebuke would be that God's standards are beyond my comprehension. But I cannot accept that a lifetime of thinking and acting, the chain of moral decisions, good and bad, is a waste of time.

I *could* accept the proposition that I will never live up to what I believe is moral and virtuous without help. I *could* accept that that belief itself might be a Maker's imprint on the clay of my head, and that the function of a true religion is to help the poor clay creature migrate back to his Maker. I know I need help to be good; but beyond being good I don't really have any ambitions. If it leads to eternal bliss, fine. But Paul's contention that all of this is pointless, just a way to bide time within the parenthesis of mortality, sounds crazy to me.

Actually, it's easy to poke fun at Paul. Scholars too seem to pick up energy when they deal with his letters. That's because, reading through *Acts* and the letters, you get, as nowhere else in the Bible, the sense of dealing with an actual character, a human personality whose moods and inconsistencies, as well as his considerable intelligence, are on display. It occurs to me that his character—his severity, his energy, his fervor, his ambitiousness, his fanatic determination—have informed our culture as much as his beliefs.

Paul wrote *Romans* just before his last visit to Jerusalem, around 57 CE. Deciding that he had accomplished as much among the contentious Turks and Greeks as he was going to, he was planning to switch his base of operations from Asia Minor to Europe. Before that, however, he was committed to making a visit to

Jerusalem, ostensibly to deliver to donations gathered from the Asian churches. But the real reason for this visit may have been to make an effort at healing the rift between his ministry and that of John, Peter, and James.

In any case, Paul had a premonition that this was that this was a very dangerous time for him. He speaks of it openly at the end of *Romans*:

> *But I beg you, brothers, by our Lord Jesus*
> *Christ and the love of the Spirit, to help me*
> *through my dangers by praying to God for me.*
> *Pray that I may escape the unbelievers in*
> *Judaea, and that the aid I carry to Jerusalem*
> *may be accepted by the saints.*

15:30-32

And indeed after this visit he was never a free man again. As we learned in *Acts,* soon after his arrival in Jerusalem Paul was placed under arrest by the local Roman tribune. Two years later he's on his way to Rome. Two years after that he was probably crucified.

Philippians

The letter to the Phillippian church (and all the rest of Paul's letters) were written from Rome, where he was being held under house arrest.

"It would be a sign from God that he has given you the privilege not only of believing in Christ, but of suffering for him as well." (1:29-30) That's a new note, isn't it? The *privilege* of suffering. Perhaps this new emphasis on suffering was because suffering was now Paul's full-time job.

There's something softer, sweeter, more vulnerable and grateful about Paul's letters from his confinement. The authorities have got him in their clutches, finally, and now he can stop struggling. Gone is the finger-shaking moral administrator. Now he turns inward a little, and examines the substance of his own faith.

> *Life to me, of course, is Christ, but then death would bring me something more; but then again, if living in this body means doing work which is having good results—I do not know what I should choose. I am caught in this dilemma; I want to be gone and be with Christ, which would be very much the better, but for me to stay alive in this body is a more urgent need for your sake.*

1:21-25

Ephesians, Colossians, Titus, 2 Timothy, Philomon
These (except for Philomon) are letters widely doubted by scholars to have come from Paul's hand or dictation. One presumes they come from disciples or associates of Paul and, reading them, you can get the impression they are attempts to shore up areas where the business of Christianity was running into problems. Specifically, they are preoccupied with precisely that area of Paul's theology where it is most vulnerable: the control of worldly behavior.

The essence of Paul's teaching was this: First God gave us the Law, which we failed to live up to, and thus fell into a permanent state of sin. Then he sent His son, Jesus, who offered himself up as a sacrifice, accepting the burden of all human sins, past, present, and future; the only provision being that only those who had faith would be saved.

Once people accept that faith alone can save, the old Law falls away. The sins it was meant to suppress have been bought and paid for.

What incentive, therefore, does Christianity offer to restrain human behavior? Very little. Mainly these letters speak in terms of decorum, the common sense of how men and women should treat each other in order to make daily life possible.

> ***Ephesians****: "In particular, I want to urge you in the name of the Lord, not to go on living the aimless kind of life that pagans live. Intellectually they are in the dark, and they are estranged from the life of God, without knowledge because they have shut their hearts to it. Their sense of right and wrong once dulled, they have abandoned themselves to sexuality and eagerly pursue a career of indecency of every kind."*

4:17-20

> ***Colossians****: "That is why you must kill everything in you that belongs only to earthly life: fornication, impurity, guilty passion, evil desires and especially greed, which is the same thing as worshipping a false god; all this is the sort of behavior that makes God angry."*

3:5-6

The author of *Titus* brings the matter to a finer point. He reiterates that God has saved us "...not because he was concerned with any righteous actions we might have done ourselves," but "...for no reason except his own compassion." (3:5) Yet he argues that true Christians should still endeavor to lead moral lives, "so that they are in every way a credit to the teaching of God our savior." (2:10) That is, Christians should think of themselves as advertisements for Christianity. From here, it's only a small step from proselytizing, the new duty of a Christian life. ("...proclaim the message and, welcome or unwelcome, insist on it," writes the author of *2 Timothy*. [4:2])

Those Gnasty Gnostics
1 and *2 Timothy* focus on the problem of heretical teachings. Gnosticism in particular was becoming a problem. Gnosticism is a catch-all term for a sort of intellectual mysticism that believes that God can be apprehended directly and that Jesus was a purely spiritual being whose material existence was little more than an illusion. For Gnostics, Jesus' death and resurrection are not the earthshaking events Paul and the rest of the Apostles make them out to be, just indications of the transience of material existence, evidence that God is much closer than anyone thought.

Gnostics were eager to brush aside the intercession of Paul's teachings and address heaven directly. Naturally, they are not spoken of well in Paul's letters. *1 Timothy* refers to them as people "...with a craze for questioning everything and arguing about words," (6:4) people who have "...pointless philosophical discussions and antagonistic beliefs of the 'knowledge' which is not knowledge at all." (6:20-21)

Philomen
Philomon is a note, really, less than a page. At issue is a slave named Onesimus, who apparently has run away from his owner, Philemon, a Christian. Onesimus has taken refuge with Paul in prison, become a Christian convert, and in the process made

himself practically indispensable as a servant. Paul pretends to be sending him back to his owner with this note, which is a little masterpiece of personal diplomacy, because the truth is that Paul doesn't want to give him up. Listen as he hems and haws and slithers around the point:

> *Now, although in Christ I can have no diffidence about telling you to do whatever is your duty, I am appealing to your love instead, reminding you that this is Paul writing, an old man now and, what is more, still a prisoner of Christ Jesus. I am appealing to you for a child of mine, whose father I became while wearing these chains...I am sending him back to you....*[though] *I should have liked to keep him with me.... However, I did not want to do anything without your consent; it would have been forcing your act of kindness, which should be spontaneous.*

1:8-15

This man was a world-class manipulator. Just imagine if he had been a door-to-door salesman. Actually, he was.

Hebrews
No one believes Paul wrote this. But it is still associated with Paul's ministry, and, somehow, it made it into the Bible. It is called *Hebrews* because the author's rhetorical strategy is to examine in detail the function of a rabbi in order to argue that this is an earthly, flawed model of how things are done in heaven. On earth, the rabbi intercedes for the faithful by offering a sacrifice to God; in heaven, Christ as the High Priest intercedes by the eternal example of his sacrifice of Himself. Now that we have been given

access to the heavenly version of the ritual, we can stop playing with the earthly model of it. And in fact, only those who recognize this are going to be prepared when God finally comes down from the mountain to reveal His glory directly. On the other hand, those Christians to whom all this has been explained and who still find themselves unable to hold to the faith will be damned more surely than anyone else.

That last point, brought up in 10:26-31 and 12:14-17, is a new wrinkle in Pauline theology. The problem, you'll remember, is that Paul left the priests with no leverage over their congregations, no way to enforce "Godly" behavior because Christ's sacrifice had taken care of all sins. Some writers, such as Timothy, suggest that Christians should behave well because such behavior is pleasing to God; that it advertises Christianity's truth to others who might be wavering. The author of *Hebrews* tightens the nut one more turn: if you have acquired knowledge of the eternal truth and then choose to sin anyway, you will be damned beyond any possibility of redemption.

Christianity, as Paul passed it on to us, is really the announcement of a gigantic Product Recall. 'You don't work,' God is saying to humanity, 'you never have and you never will. I gave you a Law and you could not follow it, no matter how angry I got and how many chances I gave you. Then I sent my Son to redeem you. And most of you *still* aren't paying attention! That's it. I'm done. The tiny fraction of you who accept Jesus as their savior will be saved. The rest will be thrown away.' End of message.

But, unfortunately for Paul, this colossal culling didn't happen. At least not in his lifetime—and not, so far, in ours.

The Letter of James

The Letter of James was one of the last books accepted into the New Testament canon. James was Jesus' brother. He was the most conservative of the Apostles, firmly believing that he was a Jew and would always be a Jew. He believed that his brother's teachings were not the basis of a new religion, but merely a new stage in the development of Judaism. *The Letter of James* defends this position by frequently quoting from the Old Testament and asserting the primacy of the Torah as God's measure of human righteousness. The author even uses the word "synagogue" instead of "church" to denote the customary place of worship.

But its sharpest and most vigorously defended point has to do with the issue of faith versus acts. Paul, you'll remember, introduced the revolutionary idea that the Old Testament Law had failed as a vehicle for man's salvation. The central theme of Paul's teaching was that by sending his son to the earth to absorb mankind's sins, God was signaling a change in the rules—from now on, all that was required for salvation was faith in Jesus as the savior of mankind, nothing more (*Galatians* 2:15-21.) Obedience or disobedience of the Law is no longer the issue, only what a person carries in his heart.

James had problems with this concept, and openly crossed swords with Paul over the issue. *The Letter of James* takes up the argument by defending the Law as the best measure of one's commitment to faith. His strongest argument takes us (of course) back to the Old Testament, to *Genesis 22*, where Abraham is waking to his vocation as patriarch. There, Yahweh, in a test of Abraham's faith, orders him to offer up his son Isaac as a sacrifice. Only when it is absolutely clear that Abraham is prepared to kill his son, does Yahweh intervene to save the boy and reward Abraham with his blessing. Says James:

> *There you see it: faith and deeds were working together; [Abraham's] faith became perfect by what he did....You see now that it is by doing something good, and not only by believing, that a man is justified.*

2:22-25

As for people (like Paul) who want to shove the Law aside, James has this to say:

> *But if you condemn the Law, you have stopped keeping it and become a judge over it. There is only one lawgiver and He is the only judge and has the power to acquit or to sentence. Who are you to give a verdict on your neighbor?*

4:11-12

Paul would have dusted his sandals at that. "Fine," he would have said. "Be a Jew. Loser."

1 Peter

1 Peter may be the first stirring of the Roman Catholic Church. It was probably not written by Peter, but by now that hardly matters. It was written from Rome, the once and future capital of the new religion, and is addressed to congregations in the far-flung territories of Asia Minor (the area where Paul concentrated most of his missionary zeal). Its intent is to gently cast a uniform doctrinal net over the whole of its audience. So without further adieu, here it is, making its debut epistle, the *RRRoman...Catholic...**CHURCH!***

Reading *1 Peter* you can see that Christian preaching is beginning to acquire its own rhetoric. Back in Paul's days there was still a certain amount of disarray in the movement. Some of the faithful weren't sure if they were Christian or Jews. The Apostles bickered among themselves. Paul himself expressed profound disagreement with the Jerusalem patriarchs Peter and James, going so far as to call Peter a hypocrite for changing his mind about eating with gentile converts. (*Galatians* 2:11-14)

By the time *1 Peter* was written, thirty or forty years later, the Christians appear to have gotten their act together. For one thing, they're willing to call themselves Christians, a term that the real Peter had never heard of until Paul brought it from Antioch. They no longer regard themselves as a renewed form of Judaism, but as a separate religion.

They've got their own lexicon, their own symbols, their own characteristic way of blessing each other. Listen to the opening greeting of *1 Peter*:

> *Peter, apostle of Jesus Christ, sends greetings to all those living among foreigners in the Dispersion of [Asia Minor], who have been chosen, by the provident purpose of God the Father, to be made holy by the Spirit, obedient to Jesus Christ and sprinkled with his blood.*

1:1-2

Notice how smoothly now the Trinity is invoked: "God the Father...holy by the Spirit...obedient to Jesus Christ." Notice too the beginning of the Church's long love affair with the blood and suffering of Christ's Passion: "sprinkled with his blood" as a metaphor for baptism (also referred to a little later as "the precious blood of a lamb without spot or stain," [1:20]). It's as if Peter is trying to expose his provincial readers to the authorized version of their religion.

Christians are no longer confused with Jews. In fact, Peter all but asserts they have taken over the Jews' role as the Chosen People:

> *But you are **a chosen race, a royal priesthood, a consecrated nation, a people set apart** to sing the praises of God who called you out of the darkness into his wonderful light. Once you were not a people at all and now you are the People of God...*

2:9-10

The bolded phrases are quotes from the Old Testament books of *Isaiah* and *Hosea*, which Peter is now appropriating for Christian duty.

Aside from conveying a sense that the Christian Church is going to be run from Rome, Peter has another message for his brethren on the other side of the world. It is this: 'Expect to suffer just as Jesus suffered, while trying to imitate his poise and humility.'

Roman authorities regarded Christianity as a Jewish sect. As the movement gathered more followers, the Romans began to regard it as a threat. Persecution of Christians began toward the end of the first century CE. Christian leaders thought that new converts should realize what they were in for.

Thus it is that Peter stresses not only the likelihood of persecution, but the virtue of suffering for one's faith. Here we see the beginning of the hallowed Church tradition of the Imitation of Christ.

> *This, in fact, is what you were called to do,*
> *because Christ suffered for you and left an*
> *example for you to follow the way he took.*

2:21

Suffering in this way is a privilege:

> *...if you do have to suffer for being good, you*
> *will count it a blessing.... And if it is the will of*
> *God that you should suffer, it is better to suffer*
> *for doing right than for doing wrong.*

3:13-17

Besides, it doesn't last for long ("You will only have to suffer for a little while," [5:10]) and you will have all eternity to recover in the heaven that you are surely going to.

Short, smoothly written, and straightforward, *1 Peter* serves well as a brief introduction to the rigors of being a Christian around 100 CE. The letter wanders only once from its thematic line, in a strange little speculation about what Jesus might have been up to during his three days among the dead:

> *...the dead had to be told the Good News as well, so that though, in their life on earth, they had been through the judgment that comes to all humanity, they might come to God's life in the spirit.*

4:6

You can see what's happening here. The more time that goes by, the more theological difficulties arise. First it was the Thessalonians expressing their anxiety to Paul about their recent dead. His answer was that anyone who died believing in Christ would be raised up from the dead on Judgment Day. Okay, fine. But what about the dead who had never had a chance to learn about Jesus? Now Peter reveals they're taken care of as well.

But it won't end there. Dead babies, the ignorant masses in Africa, transubstantiation, the Trinity, Manichaeism, homosexuals, birth control—the list goes on and almost certainly will be added to. The Church has never been in danger of running out of spiritual problems to adjudicate.

The letter ends in a flurry of secret signs and symbols, as if to confirm everybody in the delicious conspiracy of being a Christian:

> *Your sister in Babylon, who is with you among the chosen, sends you greetings; so does my*

son, Mark.

5:13

"Your sister" is the Church, "Babylon" is Rome, the "chosen" are (now) the Christian community. And "Mark"? Mark is probably just Mark, possibly the author's amanuensis.

1, 2 & 3 John

Growing Pains
Just as a pimple denotes the onset of adolescence, heresy denotes a developmental stage in the maturation of a religion. The author of the three books of *John* (unknown to history, but certainly not the Apostle John) has detected an infection of Antichrists attempting to undermine the teachings of Jesus Christ. At issue is the nagging Gnostic problem emanating from that stubborn group of would-be Christians who maintain that Jesus was not a flesh-and-blood human being, but a purely spiritual entity. The author of *1 John* aims to put an end to all this foolishness:

> *You can tell the spirits that come from God by this: every spirit which acknowledges that Jesus the Christ has come in the flesh is from God; but any spirit which will not say this of Jesus is not from God, but is the spirit of Antichrist, whose coming you were warned about.*

1 John 4:2-3

♪Love, Love, Love, Love is All You Need♪
John's pastoral advice to the faithful is interesting because it shows that the marketing staff has radically simplified the core message. It's hard to imagine Paul, whose calling it was—piece-by-piece, crisis-by-crisis—to construct an entire religion, being comfortable with such a dumbed-down product.

John has whittled it down to four simple precepts: avoid sin; keep the commandments; distance yourself from worldly temptations; and be on guard for the Antichrist.

He made it even simpler than that. There is only *one* commandment that really counts: love one another. He really goes on about it:

> *My dear people,*
> *let us love one another*
> *since love comes from God*
> *and everyone who loves is begotten by God and*
> *knows God.*
> *Anyone who fails to love can never have known*
> *God,*
> *because God is love.*

1 John 4:7-8

Can you imagine Paul's sparking brain bobbing about in that treacle? I don't think so. But at least it's easy to understand.

2 John
This less than half-page "book" re-iterates that the Antichrist is anyone who preaches that Jesus did not come in the flesh. "You must not receive him in your house or even give him a greeting. To greet him would make you a partner in his wicked work." (1:10-11)

3 John
How this embarrassing tattle-tale note made it into the Bible is beyond me. It concerns an exchange of internecine bickering about a pushy church leader named Diotrephes who refuses to welcome John and his companions.

> *I have written a note for the members of the*
> *church, but Diotrephes, who seems to enjoy*
> *being in charge of it, refuses to accept us. So if*

I come, I shall tell everyone how he has behaved, and about the wicked accusations he has been circulating against us. As if that were not enough, he not only refuses to welcome our brothers, but prevents the other people who would have liked to from doing it, and expels them from the church.

1:9-10

This is unseemly. You're supposed to do your laundry at home, not in the Bible.

The Letter of Jude

Thisis a warning to all Christians about "Certain people [who] have infiltrated among you..." (1:4) He goes on to compare them to fallen angels and the fornicators of Sodom and Gomorrah. The target of Jude's ire was probably a charismatic movement known as the antinomians (literally: against the law) who held that their mystical grasp of the essence of Christ's godhood made them immune to sin. They were said to indulge in sexual excesses, and apparently it is this group that Jude has in mind when he says they behave "like unreasoning animals." (1:10)

Jude condemns them with a blustery brand of Old Testament rhetoric the like of which has not been seen in the Bible since *Isaiah* and *Jeremiah.*

> *May they get what they deserve, because they have followed Cain....They are like clouds blown about by the winds and bringing no rain, or like barren trees which are then uprooted in the winter and so are twice dead; like wild sea waves capped with shame as if with foam; or like shooting stars bound for an eternity of black darkness.*

1:11-14

Like so many apocalyptic writers before and since, Jude uses a group of people he finds repugnant as evidence that the world is about to come to an end:

> *But remember, my dear friends, what the apostles of our Lord Jesus Christ told you to*

> *expect. "At the end of time," they told you, "there are going to be people who sneer at religion and follow nothing but their own desires for wickedness."*

1:17-19

To his credit, the author of Jude tries to stay faithful to the principle of love. For example, he encourages his readers to save as many of these misguided Christians as seem worth saving, but:

> *...there are others to whom you must be kind with great caution, keeping your distance even from outside clothing which is contaminated by vice.*

1:23

> Outside clothing? Are we back in *Leviticus* again?

The Book of Revelation

[Editor's note: More than any other book of the Bible, Revelation *relies on symbols to tell its story. It was written around 95 CE, during a time of systematic persecution by the Roman caesars. The author of* Revelation *no doubt believed that its content was so inflammatory that it had to be written in a sort of symbolic code. There's hardly a passage that means exactly what it says. Does everybody have their decoders out? Okay, here we go.]*

If *Genesis* is the story of creation and the beginning of time, then *Revelation* is the story of the end of time and the beginning of eternity.

But who would have thought it would put the Jews back on top again? It almost seems like a joke. After the narrative has gone to all this trouble to prove that the Jews were blind to Jesus' divinity and guilty of his death, it's going to let them off the hook!

There's no question about it: *Revelation*, the book about God's final judgment, stipulates that 144,000 Jews, 12,000 from each of the twelve original Israelite tribes, are saved before the Apocalypse begins:

> *"Wait before you do any damage on land or at sea or to the trees, until we have put the seal on the foreheads of the servants of our God."*
> *Then I heard how many were sealed: a hundred and forty-four thousand, out of all the tribes of Israel."*

7:3-4

The passage goes on to list the twelve tribes of Israel, reserving 12,000 places in heaven for each one.

Imagine how the righteous Christians, standing there patiently outside the Heavenly gates, must feel as the stretch limo pulls up and a 144,000 Jews pile out and are escorted inside by security. Jesus Christ! Who do they know?

Repent, For The End is Near!
Apocalyptic writing was a popular form among Old Testament contributors. *Isaiah, Jeremiah, Ezekiel,* and *Daniel* all contain passages meant to make your hair stand up. *The Book of Revelation* continues this tradition. The writer is "John," presumably the Apostle John, who has been exiled to the island of Patmos for having too energetically preached the Word. The fearful visions of monsters and angels and devils he has while on the island constitute the substance of *Revelation.*

There is—how shall we say this?—a certain coarseness, a certain P.T. Barnum quality to *Revelation's* bombast. It's as if, in a final sweep of the Bible's audience, the editors decided to pitch it at about a sixth-grade level so as not to leave out anyone. You want the story of the end of creation acted out by superheroes, giants, and monsters? Well then, here's *Revelation.*

After some throat-clearing, John begins his visionary narrative:

> *I heard a voice behind me, shouting like a trumpet, "Write down all that you see in a book...." I turned around to see who had spoken to me, and...I saw seven golden lamp stands and, surrounded by them a figure like a Son of Man, dressed in a long robe tied at the*

> *waist with a golden girdle. His head and his hair were white as white wool or as snow, his eyes like a burning flame, his feet like burnished bronze, and his voice like the sound of the ocean. In his right hand he was holding seven stars, out of his mouth came a sharp sword, double-edged, and his face was like the sun shining with all its force.*

1:10-16

That, of course, is Jesus Christ, who presently invites John to "Come up here: I will show you what is to come in the future." (4:1-2) With that, John is immersed in a series of visions.

The first vision describes the opening of the Seven Seals. These seals each clasp a scroll on which God has written something important. The breaking of each seal is itself a theatrical event.

The first four seals release one by one the Four Riders of the Apocalypse: death by war, by starvation, by plague, and by wild beasts. Their job is to bring about the end of the world.

The opening of the fifth seal reveals the impatient hordes of souls who have been killed "on account of the Word of God." (6:9) They're anxious to move on to Paradise from whatever holding tank they've been waiting in. Each of them is given a white robe and told to be patient just a little longer.

The opening of the sixth seal sets off the first warning to those on earth that the end of the world is at hand:

> *"...there was a violent earthquake and the sun went as black as coarse sackcloth; the moon turned red as blood all over, and the stars of*

> *the sky fell on to the earth like figs*[26]..."
> 6:12-13

Then it's time to open the seventh seal. Here's the entire description of what happens:

> *The Lamb* [the codeword for Jesus Christ] *then broke the seventh seal, and there was silence in heaven for about half an hour.*
> 8:1

First we have cosmic bedlam—earthquakes, bloody moon, falling stars—then silence. That's pretty effective, after the crashing thunder and galloping death that precede it. John of Patmos knew something about dramatic timing.

Apocalyptic Olympiad
The opening of the seals essentially completes the story. The rest of *Revelation* is a slow motion instant replay showing in greater detail the extent of the destruction and its symbolic and numerological meaning. In addition to the seven seals—but before the seventh seal is broken—there are seven trumpets to be sounded signaling various cataclysmic events and seven bowls of plagues to be upturned.

Mixed in with the descriptions of these concentric punishments are a number of visionary digressions focusing on particular entities or issues important to the unfolding of events. It makes for a confusing read.

---

[26] I wonder if James Joyce was thinking of this passage when he wrote "The heaventree of stars hung with humid nightblue fruit," in Episode 17 of *Ulysses*.

In some ways the spectacle that is *Revelation* is like the Olympics, with many events running concurrently from one end of the firmament to the other. Sitting in the stands it's hard to grasp the totality of what's going on, so you tend to fix on what's happening in front of you, such as the locusts that pour into the world during the blowing of the fifth trumpet:

> *To look at, these locusts were like horses armored for battle; they had things that looked like gold crowns on their heads, and faces that seemed human, and hair like women's hair, and teeth like lions' teeth....Their tails were like scorpions', with stings...*

9:7-10

If you happen to be sitting near where that's going on, you're not going to care that much about the star called Wormwood that falls from the sky (over there, by the pole vault) or the victory ceremonies going on for some previous event (such as the "rewarding of the saints" in Chapter 7.)

There's no use in trying to make sense out of all the individual events. The intention is to give the impression of an incomprehensibly huge and violent final convulsion. John, our guide, is even instructed at one point to withhold the full meaning of one of the events—the seven thunderclaps of 10:4 whose utterance John is admonished not to write down. The narrative strategy is not to clarify and explain, but to astonish, titillate and terrify.

Can't Tell the Players without a Scorecard
The descriptions are so overlapped and re-looping that they defy summary, but it is possible to keep track of certain characters, and

that is probably the smartest way to talk about it. The central character on Heaven's side (God's role throughout being merely to authorize) is the "Lamb," AKA known as Jesus. At the other extreme of the bestiary is Satan, "a huge red dragon which had seven heads and ten horns." (12:4)

Satan is just coming off a big loss (12:7) to the archangel Michael who, doing us no favor, tosses his defeated adversary down to earth[27]. The Satanic dragon immediately begins to make war on mankind.

He causes two other beasts to appear, one, his chief lieutenant, from the sea, the other, the sea beast's assistant, from the land. These beasts personally and visibly intervene in human affairs, and their exploits are often the focus of speculation about the prophetic meaning of *Revelation*.

The land beast administers the policies of the sea beast, and together the two, with heaven's complicity, are given temporary dominion over the world:

> *For forty-two months the* [sea] *beast was*
> *allowed to mouth its boasts and blasphemies*
> *and to do whatever it wanted.... It was allowed*
> *to make war against the saints and conquer*
> *them, and given power over every race, people,*
> *language and nation...*

13:5-8
_____

[27] This moment was previewed in *Isaiah* 14:12-15: "How did you come to fall from the heavens, Daystar ["Lucifer" is the Latin translation for the Hebrew "Daystar"], son of Dawn? How did you come to be thrown to the ground, you who enslaved the nations?"

The only choice left for each person is to decide whether or not to worship the beast, and even that is not a choice, but something "written down since the foundation of the world in the book of life." [28] (13:8)

The land beast, on orders from the sea beast, announces a new program that fundamentalist Christians find especially chilling:

> *He compelled everyone—small and great, rich and poor, slave and citizen—to be branded on the right hand or on the forehead, and made it illegal for anyone to buy or sell anything unless he had been branded with the name of the beast or with the number of its name.*

13:16-17

Fundamentalists find that phrase "the number of its name" extremely threatening. Thus the Social Security System, with a number for each U.S. citizen, is the work of the beast. ATMs and PIN numbers are the work of the beast. I used to work with a person who refused to read the number of any credit card with a holographic image, because she'd been told by her pastor that packed into the hologram was all the information Satan needed to carry her to Hell. And this number is no secret. *Revelation* is quite open about it:

---

[28] One of the cultural beliefs we have manifestly *not* inherited from the Bible is the belief that free will plays a crucial part in the soul's journey. Time and again the Biblical narrative sets up situations where men were being condemned for doing what Yahweh was making them do. Remember the poor Pharaoh in *Exodus*, who couldn't have been nice to the Jews even if he had wanted to? Of him Yahweh says: "I myself will harden his heart, and he will not let the people go." (4:21)

> *There is no need for shrewdness here: if
> anyone is clever enough he may interpret the
> number of the beast: it is the number of a man,
> the number 666.*

13:18

And who might that be? Actually it's pretty clear who it is. John of Patmos' native language was Aramaic but he wrote in Greek, the way learned Englishmen once wrote in Latin. In those days all letters did double-duty as numbers, a practice that continued until the Arabs introduced specialized numerals to Europeans. Written in Greek (רסק נורנ), the number six hundred and sixty-six works out to the name NERO CAESAR, probably the most odious of the persecuting Caesars.

Scholars place the date of *Revelation's* composition in the mid-90s CE. Nero is reported to have committed suicide in 68 CE, and soon after there was a widespread rumor that he was not really dead but about to come back at the head of a new bloodthirsty army. That, say scholars, is the dread legend that John was working up into a cosmological conspiracy. For those who believe literally in the Bible, this is not an intellectual exercise, but a matter of eternal life or death, for directly from heaven comes the word:

> *"All those who worship the beast and his
> statue, or have had themselves branded on the
> hand or forehead, will be made to drink the
> wine of God's fury...and the smoke of their
> torture will go up forever and ever."*

14:9-11

True Christians are expected to prefer death to cooperating with the beast. Problem is, what constitutes cooperation? A bank card, a Social Security card?

This brings us to the famous "grapes of wrath" passage (foreshadowed in *Isaiah* 63), which deserves to be savored for its horrific compression. It is the Day of Judgment, and the righteous souls are being harvested and gathered up to heaven. As Isaiah tells it, an avenging angel equipped with a "sharp sickle" has just been released from the Temple in Heaven to descend upon those who have rejected salvation. He gets his orders:

> *"Put your sickle in and cut all the bunches off the vine of the earth; all its grapes are ripe." So the angel set his sickle to work on the earth and harvested the whole vintage of the earth and put it into a huge winepress, the winepress of God's anger, outside the city, where it was trodden until the blood that came out of the winepress was up to the horses' bridles as far away as sixteen hundred furlongs.*

14:18-20

That's a lot of blood.

Revelation's schizophrenic narrative drops the theme of the beasts for a chapter or two in order to fix its murderous eye on the city of Rome itself, here called "Babylon the Great, the mother of all the prostitutes." (17:5)[29] But after Rome is thoroughly trampled and

---

[29] A fascinating note on this passage in Harper's Bible Commentary says that the description of the prostitute ("I saw a woman riding a scarlet beast") may derive from illustrations engraved on Roman coins of the time. The coins reproduced the image of Vespasian, the goddess Rome, seated on Rome's seven

the victory exulted over ("Alleluia! The smoke of her will go up forever and ever." [19:3]) the narrative returns to the rolling thunder of the Apocalypse's main business, the destruction of the world. Next event: the Millennium.

Finally, Hell!
The ground rules for the Millennium are simple. First there is a great battle (19:11-21), the one at Armageddon presumably, where all the unholy kings were gathered in 16:16. Suddenly Christ bursts through the sky arrayed in his battle-gear, at the head of "the armies of heaven on white horses." (19:15) The two evil beasts are thrown into "the fiery lake of burning sulphur" (19:20), and that's the end of them—or rather the beginning of their eternal torture.

Here is Hell's formal entrance into the New Testament, though we've known all along it's been coming. Much of what we first read in *Isaiah* percolates up through *Revelation*, and here the metaphor first implied by descriptions of the offal-pit known as the Valley of Ben Hinnom, located outside the walls of Jerusalem— referred to by Isaiah as Topheth (30:32) and by Jesus as Gehenna (Mark 9:43-48)—has now reached its full fruition as Hell.

Meanwhile the Head Beast, the seven-headed dragon (Satan), is locked up in a different place, the "Abyss," a purgatory-like place where the unjudged dead lie. There he is sentenced to stay for a thousand years. During this millennium Christ personally rules the earth with the help of the martyrs, who have been patiently waiting ever since they were given their white robes back in Chapter 6. <u>This is the Millennium that fundamentalist Christians talk so much</u>

---

hills, with the river god Tiber reclining at her right, and the she-wolf with Romulus and Remus at the lower left. Think of John bent over his scroll, pen in hand, staring at the coin, fuming with imagery.

about. We're still waiting for it to begin. When it ends, after the thousand years are up, Satan is released and attacks again, suffers his final defeat, and is tossed into the fiery lake where his cohorts await him.

Don't forget that all this happens (if we're to make *any* sense of John's chronology) between the opening of the sixth and seventh scrolls. But now we've caught up with ourselves. Once again we're at the end, the moment we've already visited when "there was silence in heaven for about half an hour." This time John gives us a better picture of what's going on, what spectacle it is that silences the heavenly host. It is nothing less than the Judgment, the moment of truth for all earthly souls, the moment when:

> *"Death and Hades were emptied of the dead*
> *that were in them; and everyone was judged*
> *according to the way in which he had lived."*

20:13-14

The dignified, almost legalistic restraint of that phrasing befits its role as the most solemn moment in the New Testament, even though it directly contradicts the teachings of Paul and Peter, who emphasized that faith alone is sufficient for salvation. Apparently, it's not. Don't argue. This is the Bible.

An obvious question is, why have the Millennium at all? Why not just defeat Satan and the two beasts once and then get straight to the business of the Resurrection and the Judgment?

The answer seems to lie in the writer's desire to placate as many traditions as possible in his story of how creation ends. You'll notice that he empties "Death" (the Jewish Sheol, the timeout place) and "Hades" (the Greek underworld)[30] as all humankind prepares itself for new lodgings in either Heaven or Hell. Recognizing, at least, these afterlives from other traditions, he brings them into the Christian scheme of things.

Similarly, the device of the Millennium satisfies the historical obsession of the Jews for the restoration of the House of David at the head of the world order. It doesn't do it *exactly*, not point-for-point, but it comes close enough. Jesus had always claimed (or it was claimed for him in the Gospels) to be of the line of David, thus fulfilling the basic requirement for the Messiah. But the Jews had been taught to expect a king, a great military leader. The Jesus of the Gospels, the man that turned his cheek when he was struck, who rolled his eyes on the cross, lacked the majesty and authority they were looking for.

Now here at the beginning of the Millennium the Jews get the Messiah they had always imagined. It's Jesus, of course, but this time dressed up as a sort of Super King David.

> *His eyes were flames of fire, and his head was crowned with many coronets...his cloak was soaked in blood....From his mouth came a sharp sword to strike the pagans with; he is the one who will rule them with an iron scepter, and tread out the wine of the Almighty God's fierce anger. On his cloak and on his thigh there was a name written: The King of kings and the Lord of lords.*

19:12-16

Then suddenly it's over—the Tribulation, the Millenium, the

---

[30] The Catholic church will later give us a third choice: Purgatory.

Resurrection, the Judgment—it's all yesterday's news. The door clanks shut forever over the dragon and his beasts in Hell. Those remanded to Sheol and Hades are confined in there as well, along with all the dead who didn't pass muster for Heaven. The experiment with mortality is over. One can imagine another moment of profound silence.

> *Then I saw a new heaven and a new earth; the first heaven and the first earth had disappeared now, and there was no longer any sea.*

21:1-2

It happens so fast, it's easy to miss. The Big Eraser just went across the blackboard, there, and a new creation is in place. The angelic inhabitants of a new earth are just opening their eyes. A shining new Jerusalem descends majestically, one in which "God lives among men" (21:3) and death no longer exists (though it is still possible to get tossed down to the burning lake if you misbehave.) Odd that the text specifies that this new creation, this heaven, doesn't include a sea. If you thought Heaven was going to include weekends at the beach, you're out of luck. Maybe that has something to do with John of Patmos being exiled on an island.

John provides a denouement in which an angel takes him on a tour of the New Jerusalem, which is made entirely of gold and jewelry (walls of diamond, pearly gates). The walls are 12,000 furlongs (1,367 miles) on a side. Its architecture is a careful melding of Jewish and Christian symbols. There are twelve gates for the original tribes of Israel, and twelve foundation stones for the Jesus' apostles. Clearly, the aim of *Revelation* throughout was to enfold Jewish and Christian iconography into a single myth that would unite all Yahweh's worshippers.

In the end, we're all one big happy family—except for the masses screaming in Hell. That's your religious heritage, folks. Deal with it.

Made in United States
Troutdale, OR
05/04/2024

19648172R00176